West Country Rogues and Outlaws

GERALD NORRIS

DEVON BOOKS

First published in Great Britain in 1986 by Devon Books

ISBN: 0 86114–789–8

British Library Cataloguing-in-Publication Data

Norris, Gerald
West country rogues and outlaws
1. Outlaws — England — West Country — Biography
I. Title
364.1′55′0922 HV6453.G72W4/

Printed and bound in Great Britain by A. Wheaton & Co. Ltd

DEVON BOOKS
Official Publisher to Devon County Council

Devon Books is a division of A. Wheaton & Co. Ltd, which represents:

Editorial, Design, Publicity, Production and Manufacturing
A. Wheaton & Co. Ltd
Hennock Road, Marsh Barton, Exeter, Devon EX2 8RP
Tel: 0392 74121; Telex 42749 (WHEATN G)
(A. Wheaton & Co. Ltd is a member of the
Pergamon/B.P.C.C. Group of Companies)

Sales and Distribution
Town & Country Books, P.O. Box 31, Newton Abbot, Devon TQ12 5AQ
Tel: 080 47 2690

Preface

Bountiful by nature, the West Country has produced over the centuries a bumper harvest of great men. A fair proportion of these, in strength of character and marked individuality, have borne the imprint of their origins: for instance, Sir Francis Drake, Sir Walter Raleigh, Richard Trevithick, Thomas Hardy and Ernest Bevin come to mind. Yet nature is rarely choosy and this distinctive West Country derring-do has not confined itself to the benefactors of mankind, but bloomed also in darker places, bringing forth a comparable abundance of *un*worthies. The following pages are devoted to a selection of such miscreants, among the most notorious that the West has known. With several it is difficult now to determine what is fact and what is legend, though some attempt has been made here to distinguish between the two. The people in this book represent a wide assortment of villainies, ranging from the West Country speciality of smuggling to the more widely adopted habit of cannibalism.

Acknowledgements

The author wishes to thank for their invaluable help Ian Maxted of the Westcountry Studies Library, Beresford Leavens, Natalie Davies, Dennis Heard, Barry Gardner of the *Lorna Doone* Society and the Reverend Christopher Willis. He is especially grateful to his good friend Geoffrey Household.

Illustrations are reproduced by permission of the following:

Colin Bowerman: p. 14
Exmoor National Park: p. 18
R. Harriss: p. 68
Dennis Heard: p. 32
Westcountry Studies Library: pp. 9, 25, 39, 41, 44, 49, 65

To Thomas H. Tratt,
fellow farmer and gentleman

Contents

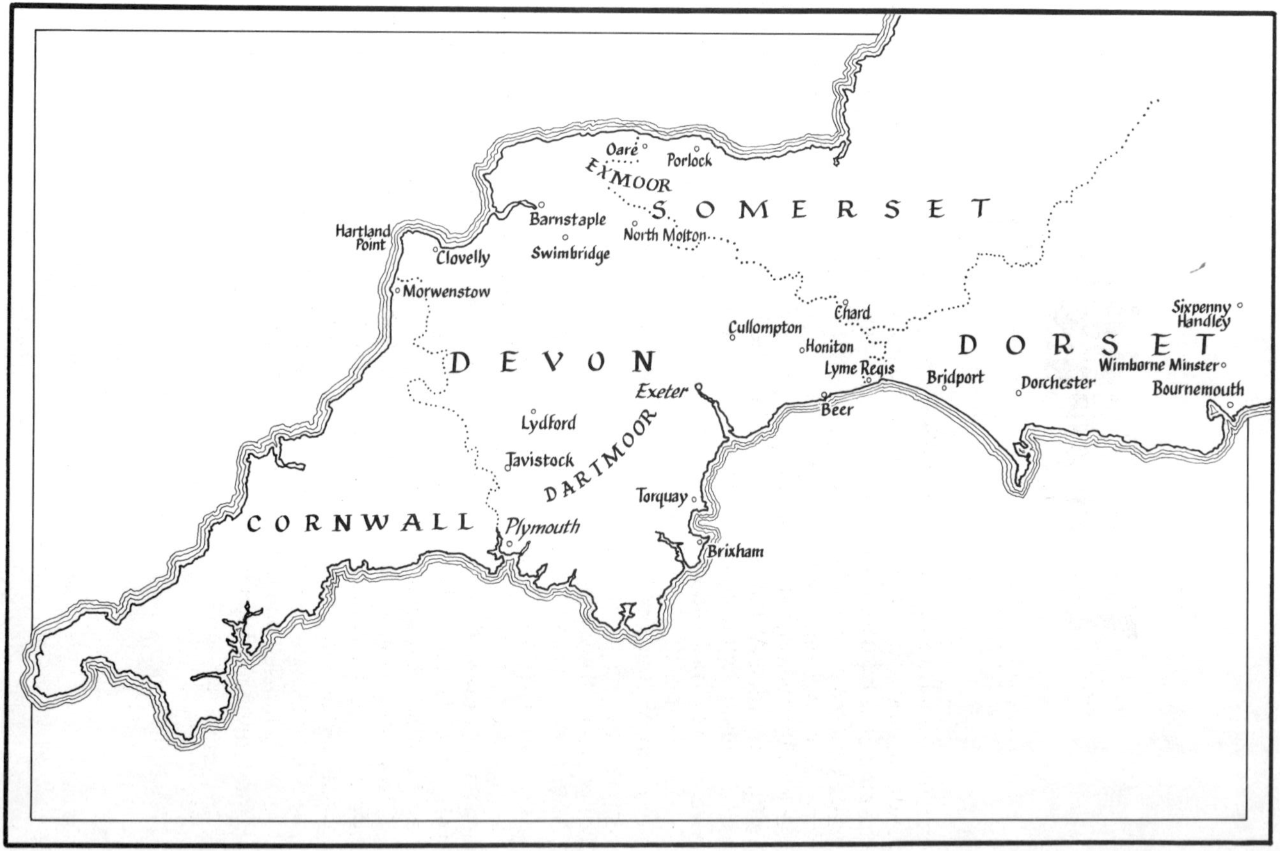

SOMERSET
DORSET
DEVON
CORNWALL
EXMOOR
DARTMOOR
Oare
Porlock
Barnstaple
North Molton
Hartland Point
Clovelly
Swimbridge
Morwenstow
Chard
Cullompton
Honiton
Lyme Regis
Beer
Bridport
Dorchester
Sixpenny Handley
Wimborne Minster
Bournemouth
Exeter
Lydford
Tavistock
Torquay
Plymouth
Brixham

1

Tom Faggus

The most renowned West Country highwayman is Tom Faggus, who seems to have been known also as Vaggus or Fergus. His escapades are well chronicled, but his existence has yet to be firmly established. He is thought to have spent his early years, around the middle of the seventeenth century, in North Molton, some twelve miles east of Barnstaple. He was initially a blacksmith; his forge stood on the edge of the village square, next to the old Poltimore Arms. At that stage of his life, there was nothing to suggest he might eventually turn to crime. However, he was drawn into an unfortunate lawsuit with the head of the powerful Bampfylde family, who resided at nearby Court Hall. As a result he was ruined, losing all his money and possessions. This reversal of fortune dealt him a further blow, since he had been on the verge of marrying his sweetheart, Betsy Paramore of South Molton. Her father cancelled the wedding and forbade her to see him again.

Heartsick and resentful, Faggus turned to highway robbery. As a blacksmith, he once won a prize at a north Devon show for the best-shod horse; now, as a highwayman, he proved equally successful. He stole from none but the rich; he never drew a drop of blood from his victims, nor treated them with violence or cruelty. His fine manners, daring, originality and cool-headedness became proverbial.

On one occasion, information was received that Faggus was riding towards Exford. Several volunteers quickly assembled and then made their way to Exford Bridge, where they waited in ambush. At length, the highwayman materialized out of the morning mist, but he had taken the precaution of disguising himself and nobody recognized him.

'Pray, my good friends,' he inquired, 'for what purpose are you gathered here in such numbers?'

'We are here to take Faggus,' they replied.

Promptly expressing his enthusiasm for their objective, he insisted on joining them; he, too, had a score to settle with that villain, he declared. After a few more minutes, he asked what firearms they possessed and, on being shown, advised them immediately to discharge and reload them, for the wet weather could well have dampened the powder and priming. They followed his suggestion without delay and fired their guns into the air, but, before they could reload, he drew out his pistols, informed them of his identity, collected their money and galloped off.

Faggus evaded capture in an even more desperate situation, when the house in which he had taken refuge in Porlock was completely surrounded. Those who lived nearby armed themselves with any weapons that came to hand: rusty old blunderbusses, muskets, scythes, pitchforks and other agricultural implements. 'Faggus is taken!' they cried, believing him to be hopelessly trapped. Suddenly his hat began to appear out of the chimney. They shot at it and it fell. An instant later, while they were reloading, the front door was flung open and the highwayman, mounted on his horse, stormed out of the house and burst through their ranks, scattering them to right and left. Astonishingly, he managed to dodge the hail of bullets and blows that threatened to annihilate him and, within another few moments, had put more than a hundred yards between himself and his gaping assailants.

Faggus's hair-raising escapes owed much to his remarkable strawberry roan, Winnie, a mare whose intelligence, fleetness of foot and devotion to her master convinced many that she possessed magic powers. In an extraordinary incident on the road outside Dulverton, when Faggus was himself held at gunpoint, Winnie suddenly reared up and with one of her forefeet dashed the pistol from the attacker's hand. Another time, the highwayman was passing a pleasant hour at the Exmoor Arms in Simonsbath, while Winnie was munching her oats in the stable. The landlord, however, had sent for constables. Soon four of them arrived and, taking Faggus completely by surprise, seized him. At once he gave a piercing whistle and a few seconds later from the stable there came sounds of splintering wood as Winnie kicked the door apart. A few more seconds and she was clattering into the hostelry and menacing the constables. Fearful for their lives, they surrendered their prisoner and scuttled for safety, leaving horse and rider free to take a leisurely departure.

The tightest spot in which Faggus and Winnie found themselves was when they were trapped on the bridge at Barnstaple. Tom had been recognized in the town a little earlier, possibly during a visit to the old Bull Inn, and word had gone out to the constables. He knew he was being followed as he headed towards Sticklepath, but as he came cantering on to Long Bridge he must have felt that any danger was past, since he could now outstrip his pursuers and make for open country. How great his surprise and consternation when he espied at the far end of the bridge a thick cordon of constables lying in wait. And, in less than no time, the officers following him out of town had arrived and sealed off the bridge behind him. So Faggus, it appeared, was in the bag at last – or undoubtedly would have been, had he not shown the most amazing presence of mind. He turned Winnie towards the parapet, spoke a quick word of encouragement and urged her forward. The incomparable strawberry mare soared into the void. Falling almost forty feet, they plummeted into the River Taw with an almighty smack that sent the spray flying higher than the bridge. Then, to the nettled disbelief of the gawking

The sixteen-span Long Bridge at Barnstaple, from which Tom Faggus and Winnie made their famous leap into the River Taw

constabulary, Winnie swiftly swam to the shore, where Faggus ceremoniously doffed a somewhat sodden hat in the direction of his audience and sped away, the water gleaming on Winnie's flanks and flicking rhythmically from her tail.

Faggus's wit was as ready as his courage. Perhaps the most pleasant instance of his humour occurred when, by coincidence, he intercepted on the road the very man, Bampfylde, whose vindictiveness in the law courts had originally reduced the young blacksmith to poverty and despair. At gunpoint, Bampfylde produced with trembling hands his heavy purse and precious ring. Faggus examined these valuables for some little while and, after making evident his regard for them, returned them to their dumbfounded owner.

'Permit me the pleasure, sir,' he remarked, 'of honouring the custom that a robber never robs a robber.'

For a man who, like Robin Hood, distributed much of his booty among the poor, and whose company was so eagerly sought by his many friends, Faggus came to what seems an unnecessarily harsh end. Officers who had been on his trail caught up with him at Exebridge, three miles south of Dulverton. He had broken his journey there and was having a drink in a tavern. One of the officers disguised himself as a beggar and went in to the room where Faggus was sitting. Displaying his habitual generosity towards those in need, Tom ordered refreshment for the feigned mendicant, who, after waiting for the right opportunity, suddenly knocked the highwayman's chair from under him.

Reinforcements immediately rushed in, overpowered Faggus, bound his ankles and hoisted him to the rafters. Despite dangling upside down several feet above the ground, he still retained sufficient composure to whistle for Winnie. But Winnie's prodigious capabilities were well known to the constabulary, and, at the very moment that her master was being strung up, she was shot. Faggus was taken to Taunton, tried and hanged. The year was apparently 1671, though it should be said that no written confirmation of the execution has been discovered.

There are a number of towns in the Exmoor area with Faggus connections. He is supposed to have spent quite a few years in Swimbridge, four miles south-east of Barnstaple, where Jack Russell was later the rector. After Faggus's arrest, his house and property were confiscated, and a royal coat of arms, fashioned in heavy cast metal, was fixed to the house, indicating its seizure. Both the house, Yeoland Cottage, and the coat of arms are still in existence. A toasting fork and a gun appear to be all that remain of the contents; they are on display at St Anne's Chapel Museum in St Peter's Churchyard, Barnstaple. Also surviving are some circular horseshoes that Faggus is said to have had forged for Winnie at a smithy in Alcombe, just south of Minehead. These are not unlike the shoes that racehorses wear; the prints that they produced would probably not have deceived Sherlock Holmes, but seventeenth-century constables might well have been deluded into misinterpreting the direction in which the horse travelled. What is thought to have been Faggus's own smithy, in North Molton, was demolished a little over sixty years ago. Land that, as a young man, he owned in Molland, five miles east of North Molton, has never been traced. But the locations of a meadow where Winnie apparently took her ease, in Combe Sydenham, four miles south of Watchet, and a stable that Faggus used in Chargot Wood, near Luxborough, have been identified. Robber's Bridge, which spans Weir Water in the Oare Valley, salutes the exploits of the dashing highwayman, yet, in reality, has no historical association with him.

Faggus is not known to have had any offspring, although claims were once made that a girl called Johanna Vaggus, who was found abandoned during the late nineteenth century in the village of Atherington, seven miles south of Barnstaple, might well have been one of his descendants. The only other relation that scholarship has unearthed was a poulterer who lived in Milk Street, Exeter.

Many people first encounter Tom Faggus when reading *Lorna Doone,* in which he plays a leading role. Blackmore introduces some of the incidents in Tom's career and creates a fascinating character whose principal traits are vivacity, restlessness and impetuosity. The Faggus of *Lorna Doone,* however, differs substantially from the Faggus of tradition: he is born later, around 1651; he marries his cousin Annie, the sister of John Ridd; he steers clear of the gallows and becomes a prosperous farmer. In Chapter 39, he further advances his situation: 'Tom Faggus returned from London very proudly and very happily, with a royal pardon in black and white, which everybody

The forge at North Molton, where Tom Faggus was believed to be the blacksmith; it was demolished in the 1920s

admired the more, because no one could read a word of it.' The idea of including Faggus in his novel may have been suggested to Blackmore by two publications in particular. The first of these was the article 'Wanderings on Exmoor' by George Tugwell, which was printed in the October 1857 edition of *Fraser's Magazine.* Here, an account of the atrocities committed by the Doones is immediately followed by a section on Faggus: 'We cannot forget, too, the wonderful history of another adventurer in those wilds – a gentleman rejoicing in the cacophonous name of "Faggus", who possessed an "enchanted strawberry horse" – an animal who was so sagacious as to do battle with hoof and teeth in his master's cause on the smallest provocation. Once the worthy pair were *in extremis* on Barnstaple Bridge, hemmed in on either side by their pursuers.' The second work that discernibly influenced Blackmore was the novella *The Doones of Exmoor,* serialized in *The Leisure Hour* during the autumn of 1863. Reference is made to Faggus in the first chapter, which appeared on 6 September. The story begins in 1641, and the highwayman is already in his grave.

> 'Marry, you're right, my lord. Old Faggus was the hero of the heath for many a long day; but he was a heart of wax compared with these gentlemen, who are more disposed than he to prove the freedom of their wills by arguments of metal.'

> 'Old Faggus, say you, colonel? What of him?'
>
> 'A bold highwayman, my lord, who scoured these wastes on a steed as famous for his fleetness and sagacity, as his master was for a remarkable combination of audacity and benevolence. He did the knave good service in many a hard pinch, and carried him safely through such dangers imminent, that he was called "The enchanted Strawberry Horse".'
>
> 'You stir my curiosity, Colonel,' said the younger cavalier. 'Let me hear some of his doings, I prithee. . . .'

Although the text is not explicit, we are led to believe that Faggus flourished in the 1560s. On the other hand, some experts maintain that he lived in neither the sixteenth century nor the seventeenth, but in the eighteenth; so there exists a wide divergence of opinion.

Blackmore's full-length portrait of Faggus has been deservedly acclaimed. Yet no less memorable is his depiction of Winnie, notably in the celebrated scene in Chapter 10 when the fifteen-year-old John Ridd is given the ride of his life, as he desperately tries to avoid being thrown. With this excerpt, let us say goodbye to Faggus the daredevil highwayman and his 'enchanted' steed.

> All the long swift while, without power of thought, I clung to her crest and shoulders, and dug my nails into her creases, and my toes into her flank-part, and was proud of holding on so long, though sure of being beaten. Then in her fury at feeling me still, she rushed at another device for it, and leaped the wide water-trough sideways across, to and fro, till no breath was left in me. The hazel-boughs took me too hard in the face, and the tall dog-briars got hold of me, and the ache of my back was like crimping a fish; till I longed to give up, and lay thoroughly beaten, and lie there and die in the cresses. But there came a shrill whistle from up the home-hill, where the people had hurried to watch us; and the mare stopped as if with a bullet; then set off for home with the speed of a swallow, and going as smoothly and silently. I never had dreamed of such delicate motion, fluent, and graceful, and ambient, soft as the breeze flitting over the flowers, but swift as the summer lightning. I sat up again, but my strength was all spent, and no time left to recover it; and at last, as she rose at our gate like a bird, I tumbled off into the mixen.

2

John Barnes

The innkeeper-turned-highwayman John Barnes, in contrast to Tom Faggus, seems rather a bleak and unglamorous figure. Yet his brief tale, with its grainy realism and tinge of fatalism, has survived alongside the spectacular episodes that embellish the career of his famous contemporary.

For much of the 1670s, Barnes was taverner at the Black Horse in South Street, Exeter, near the old South Gate and Holy Trinity Church. During that time, his wife, Mary, bore him at least three children, bringing the size of their family to about eight or nine. She was generally reckoned a virtuous and pious woman; she also had a reputation for being hard-working and thrifty, which, no doubt, she needed to be. Barnes himself was well esteemed, an ardent Presbyterian and a zealous attender of conventicles and other Nonconformist gatherings. He appears to have been a man of strong principles and was prosecuted in the Exeter diocesan court for refusing to present his children for baptism.

Around 1677, he and his family moved from the Black Horse to an inn in Cullompton, twelve miles north-east of Exeter. At that time he evidently experienced some form of inner crisis which entirely altered his view of the world. We cannot tell whether his ordeal precipitated his departure from Exeter or, conversely, whether his transformation was brought about by a change of environment. Nevertheless, whichever way it was, the outcome proved disastrous. His religious fervour abated, and, from being almost a fanatic, he swung with comparable intensity in the opposite direction. He became dissolute, extravagant, unreliable and mendacious; he began to run up large debts. One of his chief creditors was a blacksmith, an excellent man whom he continually denied reparation and who grew increasingly anxious about his own state of affairs. Matters reached a head in the summer of 1678 when, after the blacksmith had made yet another plea for the return of his money, Barnes suggested that they enter into partnership and not only resolve their respective financial difficulties, but become wealthy men into the bargain. Drawing perhaps on a fund of eloquence and impassioned rhetoric which he had absorbed at religious meetings, he totally overcame the blacksmith's scruples and persuaded him to undertake a robbery. And, not content with leading one individual astray, he prevailed upon a worsted comber to join them in their villainy. His ambitious plan was to intercept the Exeter carrier on its journey to London. This coach transported huge sums of money, which were under the protection of able and seasoned guards, and it travelled swiftly. Barnes determined to waylay it on the long steep hill that leads out of Honiton towards Chard. In those days, the road climbed through desolate countryside, which was almost completely uninhabited. It had the further advantage, as far as Barnes and his accomplices were concerned, of being sufficiently distant from Cullompton – about twelve miles – to make the possibility of recognition extremely unlikely.

Through contacts in Exeter, Barnes was evidently able to ascertain not only the date on which the next large transportation of money was to take place, but the time when the coach could be expected to reach the hill. Honiton was a major staging post and, from what we know of coach schedules at that time, it seems probable that the carriers stopped there overnight, resuming their trip shortly before dawn. The ascent of the hill may even have been undertaken in twilight, which would have suited the robbers better still. To lessen the horses' burden, the guards would have alighted at the bottom of the hill and walked beside the coach to the top. They and the coach were thus particularly vulnerable and when Barnes and his henchmen suddenly sprang from their cover virtually no resistance was offered. The guards were held at gunpoint, the money was located and loaded onto the horses, and the gang were soon riding off down the hill. Their haul turned out to be as

The hill outside Honiton where John Barnes committed his fateful robbery. Daniel Defoe described the view from here as 'the most beautiful landskip in the world'.

substantial as anything they might have desired, amounting to £600, enough to set up each of them for the rest of his days.

But Barnes's debut as a highwayman was marred by one serious oversight. He may have been resident in Cullompton, the robbery may have been committed a dozen miles away, in the middle of nowhere, but he was still well remembered in Exeter, and Exeter was the city from which the carriers came. And more than one of them had recognized him. They gave no indication at the time, since they were fearful for their lives; yet, once home again, they supplied the authorities with evidence that was overwhelmingly conclusive. The innkeeper and his colleagues were arrested and conducted to Exeter prison.

They were plainly resourceful men, because, within a short space of time, they managed to escape from the prison by night. The blacksmith appears to have freed himself from his fetters and broken enough of his comrades' shackles for them to join him in the breakout. He then succeeded in getting away altogether, but the others, still partially encumbered by their irons, were soon afterwards recaptured. Barnes endured this setback stoically. The worsted comber, however, bemoaned his fate, weeping and wailing, pleading that he had been duped into participating for the first time in an act that was alien to his nature and scruples.

At the county assizes held in Exeter on 5 August 1678 both robbers were found guilty, after the clearest possible evidence had been presented against them. They were sentenced to death. A group of ladies from some of the city's most prominent families petitioned the court to spare Barnes because of concern for his wife and many children. Their plea was rejected. The date of the execution was set for 13 August.

During his last night in prison, Barnes spent two hours praying with his family and several ministers. There is little doubt that he was now his former self, conscientious and devout. On his final day, he went calmly to the place of execution, which was possibly the Heavitree gallows. In the midst of mounting the scaffold, he stopped, turned to those who had gathered beneath and addressed them with warmth and obvious sincerity. He confessed not only to the crime for which he had been convicted, but for sundry other sins, especially that of hypocrisy. He earnestly begged the spectators for their prayers, exhorting them never to despair, whatever their situation. They should trust in the providence of God, rather than seek to answer their needs, however pressing those might seem, in ways that were not wholly upright. That, he said, is what he should have done; his failure to act correctly had brought him to this untimely end. After these remarks, voiced in a spirit of true penitence, he resumed his progress up the ladder and came face to face with the hangman. Moments later, the innkeeper who very briefly turned highwayman, had passed from this world.

3

The Doones

The Doone Valley, the Doone Gate, Lorna Doone Farm, the Doones' Warpath and other familiar Exmoor sites and landmarks perpetuate the legend of the hellish family who committed numerous atrocities during the seventeenth century. We know of the Doones principally through R. D. Blackmore's celebrated novel *Lorna Doone*, which was published in 1869. Before then, little had been written about them; nothing survives from the seventeenth and eighteenth centuries though Doone stories circulated by word of mouth in the Exmoor area during the early nineteenth century.

The first book to mention them seems to be *A Guide Containing a Short Historical Sketch of Lynton, Lynmouth, Ilfracombe, and Places Adjacent in North Devon* by Thomas Henry Cooper, printed in Barnstaple in 1853. The following extract is possibly the basis of many later accounts.

> Bagworthy or Badgeworthy, as it is called by the peasants, has for years, as we have seen, been the name of a portion of land in this parish. It lies on the side of the parish adjoining Somersetshire, and connected with this spot are various traditions of the doings of a daring and successful band of robbers, called '*The Doones of Bagworthy*' who seem to have taken up their residence there about the period of the Commonwealth. Situated among the extensive tracts of hills which surround Exmoor, far from the habitation of man, and until its enclosure in 1820, scarcely known to any but the half barbarous shepherd, or the adventurous sportsman, stands the wood of Bagworthy . . .
>
> The ruins of a village long forsaken and deserted, stand in an adjacent valley, which before the destruction of the timber must have been a spot exactly suited to the wants of the wild inhabitant. Tradition relates that it consisted of eleven cottages, and that here the 'Doones' took up their residence, being the terror of the country for many miles round. For a long time they were in the habit of escaping with their booty across the wild hills of Exmoor, to Bagworthy, where few thought it safe, or even practicable to follow them. They were not natives of this part of the country, but having been disturbed by the Revolution from their homes, suddenly entered Devonshire and erected the village

alluded to. It was known from the first to the inhabitants of the neighbouring parishes, that this village was erected and inhabited by robbers, but the fear, which their deeds inspired in the minds of the peasants, prevented them from attacking and destroying it. The idea is prevalent that before their leaving home, they had been men of distinction and not common peasants. The site of a house may still be seen on a part of the forest, called the Warren, which is said to have belonged to a person styled 'The Squire', who was robbed and murdered by the Doones.

A farm house called Yenworthy, lying just above Glenthorne, on the left of the Lynton and Porlock road, was beset by them one night; but a woman firing on them from one of the windows, with a long duck gun, they retreated, and blood was tracked the next morning for several miles in the direction of Bagworthy. The gun was found at Yenworthy and purchased by the Rev. W. S. Halliday. They entered and robbed a house at Exford in the evening before dark, and found there only a child, whom they murdered; a woman servant, who was concealed in the oven, is said to have heard them say to the unfortunate infant, the following barbarous couplet:–

'If any one asks, who kill'd thee,
'Tell'm 'twas the Doones of Bagworthy.'

It was for this murder, that the whole county rose in arms against them, and going to their abode in great haste and force, succeeded in taking into custody the whole gang, who soon after met with the punishment due to their crimes.

Cooper is thought to have drawn on manuscript versions of Doone stories then in the possession of the Reverend J. F. Chanter. These were based on interviews with Ursula Fry, who died in 1856 at the age of 90, and Aggie Norman, who died in 1860 at the age of 83, each of whom learnt her Doone yarns from Ursula Johnson, who was born into the Babb family in 1738 and died in 1826. The Babbs were for many years servants in the de Wichehalse household in Lynton.

After Cooper's guide came a book entitled *Legends of the West Country* (1854), in which reference was again made to the Doones:

The Doones of Badgworthy were a gang of bloodthirsty robbers who haunted the roads of Exmoor about the reign of Charles I, and ravaged the whole country around. Many tales are still extant of their daring and ferocity. There is a popular belief that they were men of high rank in life who, after being turned out of their homes at the conclusion of the Civil War, chose this disreputable mode of earning their bread . . .

Legends of the West Country was followed, in 1857, by two further publications that alluded to the Doones. *The North Devon Hand-Book*, edited

Badgworthy Water, on the border between Somerset and Devon, in the heart of Doone Country – 'as full of fish as of pebbles', wrote R. D. Blackmore

by George Tugwell, repeats, almost word for word, what had appeared earlier, but in the October number of *Fraser's Magazine* Tugwell's article, *Wanderings on Exmoor*, presents some additions to the familiar narrative.

> . . . there was a little child and a servant girl remaining, whose fate was quickly determined. The girl being more discreet than valorous, left her charge at the first token of danger, and hid herself in the neighbouring oven, which was of patriarchal size, and for her own sake, we may trust was not hot. From her hiding-place she heard the remainder of the story. The Doones being hungry, and not over nice, and, moreover, not succeeding in their extempore forage in kitchen and storehouse, laid hands on the unfortunate infant, cooked him, and eat him, with much unction and dispatch; and whilst they washed down his remnants with some of his father's old ale, chanted the following refrain, by way, we may suppose, of dirge and epitaph:–
>
> *If any one asks who 'twas that eat thee,*
> *Tell them – the Doones of Badgeworthy.*

The Doones made their debut as characters in romantic fiction on 5 September 1863, when the weekly magazine *The Leisure Hour* introduced the first instalment of a 22 000-word anonymous novella, *The Doones of Exmoor*. This work, which ran for eight issues, is curiously titled, since the Doones are exterminated during the fourth of the twelve chapters. In addition, none of them is individually characterized. The novella is chiefly about the de Wichehalse family and draws on stories surrounding them; it is set at the time of the Civil War, the Doones being overthrown in January 1642. The handling of the child's murder gives us the flavour of this rather dull tale. Here, it is reported to Sir Edward de Wichehalse and Lord Auberley by the landlady of The Red Lion at Lynton.

> 'There was no one at home but a little child and the maid, and when they had examined every room, and collected what money, plate, and valuables they could find, a consultation was held, and the inhuman wretches determined to prevent information being given against them, by putting the two poor things that had been left at home to death. The servant girl overheard what they said, and hid herself in the out premises; so they killed the little innocent boy.'
>
> 'Can this be true?' said Lord Auberley.
>
> 'It is, my lord,' the woman replied. 'The owner of the house and father of the child was over here this morning. The poor man is full of trouble, as well he may be, and his wife is almost beside herself.'
>
> 'It's high time,' said De Wichehalse, 'that something should be done to rid the country of these desperadoes, who will become more and more daring as they find themselves unchecked. I'll see if strength enough cannot be brought together to bring them to justice.'
>
> 'May I ask, as a special favour,' remarked Auberley, 'that you will postpone your expedition for a few weeks, until I am able to join it?'

The Doones of Exmoor has a certain importance, for it prompted *Lorna Doone*. The Reverend Dr J. Charles Cox wrote in *The Daily Chronicle* of 8 July 1903, 'I had a letter from Mr R. D. Blackmore, soon after his immortal work was issued, wherein he acknowledged that it was the accidental glancing at the poor stuff in the *Leisure Hour* that gave him the clue for the weaving of the romance, and caused him to study the details on the spot.'

Blackmore started the novel early in 1867 and completed it during April 1868. He offered the work to several magazines for serialization, but none was interested. Neither were book publishers especially enthusiastic, and when Sampson Low eventually issued the novel in three volumes on 1 April 1869, the run was limited to 500. The edition took more than two years to sell and a number of copies had to be remaindered. However, an extraordinary stroke of luck suddenly turned *Lorna Doone* into a bestseller. On 10 October 1870, the engagement was announced between the Queen's fourth daughter, Princess Louise, and the Marquess of Lorne, son of the Duke of Argyll. The Marquess had no ties with the royal family and, because this was not an arranged marriage but a true love match, people were captivated by the young couple's romance. During the five months culminating in the wedding at Windsor on 21 March 1871, numerous articles and reports about the princess and her handsome fiancé were eagerly devoured. In these circumstances, it was not long before Lorna Doone's kinship with the Lornes was brought to the public's attention. One can readily appreciate the publicity value of a passage such as the following, from Chapter 66, in which the furrier Ramsack tells John Ridd about Lorna's lineage.

> 'Perhaps you think, Master Ridd, that because her ladyship, Lady Lorna Dugal, is of Scottish origin, therefore her birth is not as high as of our English nobility. If you think so, you are wrong, sir. She comes not of the sandy Scotch race, with high cheekbones, and raw shoulder-blades, who set up pillars in their courtyards. But she comes of the very best Scotch blood, descended from the Norsemen. Her mother was of the very noblest race, the Lords of Lorne; higher even than the great Argyle, who has lately made a sad mistake, and paid for it most sadly. And her father was descended from the King Dugal, who fought against Alexander the Great. No, no, Master Ridd; none of your promiscuous blood, such as runs in the veins of half our modern peerage.'

Sampson Low quickly responded to their good fortune by producing a second edition of *Lorna Doone* in a single volume and at a reduced price of six shillings. This at once proved immensely successful. On 31 January 1870, Blackmore was able to write to the magazine publisher John Blackwood about the 'great rush upon Lorna'. After Princess Louise's wedding the novel continued to prosper. By the beginning of 1873 it had progressed to a sixth edition. Its popularity during the author's lifetime never waned; in 1897, three years before his death, all 100 000 copies of a new sixpenny edition were sold within a week of publication. Blackmore, a modest man, never forgot the happy coincidence of the royal engagement and, addressing his heroine in the preface to the twentieth edition, in 1882, wrote, '. . . a certain auspicious event occurred just then, and gave you golden wings. The literary public found your name akin to one which filled the air, and as graciously as royalty itself, endowed you with imaginary virtues. So grand is the luck of time and name . . .'

The novel soon took its place among the Victorians' best loved books. One consequence was the increasing number of girls who were christened Lorna. Another was the gathering influx of enthusiasts to that region of Exmoor in which Blackmore set his story and which he described so lyrically. Hitherto, the area had been frequented only by an occasional shepherd or hunter and was usually quite deserted. In *Exmoor Memories* (1926), Arthur Bradley relates that the forays of the first Doonatics were greeted by local inhabitants with bewilderment.

> There was no talk of Doones on Exmoor in my day . . . As their lair, suppositious or otherwise, which I believe hundreds of people still visit annually, was in the neighbouring parish, it would seem impossible but that traditions of them should not have lingered in the memory of our

old people, had there been any to linger. The Rector [of Windycombe], who was keenly alive to the folklore of the country and knew every soul on this half of the moor, had certainly never heard of them . . . Mr Russell [the Reverend Jack Russell, the terrier breeder], who knew every yard of Exmoor and everyone abiding on it, was equally unconscious of those shadowy folk who were suddenly established as the *genii* of this particular wild.'

Bradley and the rector were out riding near Brendon one morning 'in the early spring of 1870, I think it was', when they were amazed to espy two men approaching on foot. These proved to be the Reverend George Ridding, headmaster of Winchester College, accompanied by an assistant master, who was a relative of the rector's.

> 'Where on earth are you going?' said the Rector when he had recovered from his astonishment.
>
> 'To the Doone Valley,' said Dr Ridding. 'And no doubt you can put us on the right line.'
>
> 'To the *what*?' cried the Rector.
>
> 'The valley of the Doones,' repeated the other rather shortly, as if the suggestion of a joke in the Rector's tone was uncalled for.
>
> 'Never heard of such a place,' said the latter.
>
> 'What!' cried the famous headmaster, a little irritably. 'Why the whole world's ringing with it. I suppose you have heard of the Doones?'
>
> 'Never in my life,' said the Rector, laughing.
>
> 'Good gracious!' exclaimed in one voice the two adventurers.
>
> 'Then I suppose you've never read *Lorna Doone*!' almost shouted the relative, pulling a book out of his haversack and tapping it.
>
> 'Never heard of it,' said the Rector, looking enquiringly at me, who, fresh from the outer world, as it were, might conceivably save our faces.
>
> But neither my college acquaintances nor my people at home had ever mentioned this book, epoch-making as it proved, so far as Exmoor was concerned. Indeed, none of my college friends had ever so much as heard of Exmoor, as I had naturally good reason to know. It was of no use, and we had to confess that we knew nothing about *Lorna Doone* or any Blackmore, except a rather eccentric old parson at High Bray.

The early devotees of the novel, like Ridding and his companion, were responsible for locating to their own satisfaction the places mentioned in the story. Hoccombe Combe was adopted as the Doone Valley, based on John Ridd's statement in Chapter 7 that 'Bagworthy water ran out of Doone valley, a mile or so from the mouth of it'. For a time the valley was better known as Doone Glen, a name that Blackmore himself was still using in *Slain by the Doones* (1895). Most of the guidebooks initially acknowledged Hoccombe Combe to be the Doone Valley, following the lead of the Ordnance Survey, who had consulted Lord Ebrington, owner of the land in that area. However, in the *Tourist's Guide to North Devon and the Exmoor District* (1880), R.N.Worth wrote, 'The stream which flows through the Doone Valley, the Badgeworthy Water, issues from the glen by what has been aptly called the "Waterslide".' This suggests that Lank Combe, where the Waterslide is situated, was also already being accepted as the Doone Valley, in preference to Hoccombe Combe. Blackmore never allowed himself to be drawn into pronouncing on the matter. During the preparation of the 1887 *Baedeker*, he was sent a page proof that stated, 'Readers of *Lorna Doone* will be disappointed if they expect to find a close resemblance between the descriptions of the book and the actual facts of nature.' In his reply, dated 10 March 1887, he told the editor, James Muirhead, 'When I wrote *Lorna Doone* the greatest effort of my imagination would have been to picture its success. If I had dreamed that it ever would be more than a book of the moment, the descriptions of scenery – which I know as well as I know my garden – would have been kept nearer to their fact. I romanced therein, not to mislead any other, but solely for the uses of my story.'

In 1971, the Ordnance Survey caused a sensation by withdrawing the Doone Valley from its maps and letting Hoccombe Combe return to being simply Hoccombe Combe. Instead, there now emerged 'Doone Country', occupying the area bounded to the north by Lank Combe, to the south by Hoccombe Combe and to the east by Badgworthy Water. This alteration could be held to endorse the reasonable view that Blackmore used the whole Badgworthy area to provide the features of his valley. Nevertheless, the change seems to have been the resolution of a quandary into which the Ordnance Survey was precipitated once the *Lorna Doone* expert Sir Atholl Oakeley had produced overwhelming proof, three years beforehand, that Lank Combe should be recognized as the Doone Valley. It is believed that the mapmakers were totally convinced by his arguments, but were anxious not to provoke a public outcry by appearing to promote a rival to the traditional valley. 'They are in a cleft stick,' Sir Atholl told *The Daily Telegraph* on 3 May 1971. 'They cannot continue the inaccuracy of Hoccombe after agreeing I was right, and they don't want objections to Lank Combe when the new maps come out.'

Despite much disparaging criticism and being branded as a 'long-winded old concocter of romantic crudities' (according to W.W. Joyce in *Echoes of Exmoor*, published in 1926), Blackmore was a considerable scholar and a painstaking artist, who was always exceedingly careful in his historical research. He also spent his entire youth on or around Exmoor and was steeped in its folklore and legends. We should therefore not neglect to hear what he has to say about the intriguing and important issue of the Doones' origin, which is recounted by John Ridd at the start of Chapter 5 in the novel.

> In or about the year of our Lord 1640, when all the troubles of England were swelling to an outburst, great estates in the north country were

suddenly confiscated, through some feud of families, and strong influence at Court, and the owners were turned upon the world, and might think themselves lucky to save their necks. These estates were in co-heirship, joint-tenancy I think they called it, although I know not the meaning, only so that if either tenant died, the other living, all would come to the live one, in spite of any testament.

One of the joint owners was Sir Ensor Doone, a gentleman of brisk intellect; the other owner was his cousin, the Earl of Lorne and Dykemont.

Lord Lorne was some years the elder of his cousin Ensor Doone, and was making suit to gain severance of the cumbersome joint-tenancy, by any fair apportionment, when suddenly this blow fell on them, by wiles and woman's meddling; and instead of dividing the land, they were divided from it.

The nobleman was still well-to-do, though crippled in his expenditure; but as for the cousin, he was left a beggar, with many to beg from him. He thought that the other had wronged him, and that all the trouble of law befell through his unjust petition. Many friends advised him to make interest at Court, for having done no harm whatever, and being a good Catholic, which Lord Lorne was not, he would be sure to find hearing there, and probably some favour. But he, like a very hot-brained man, although he had long been married to the daughter of his cousin (whom he liked none the more for that), would have nothing to say to any attempt at making a patch of it, but drove away with his wife and sons, and the relics of his money, swearing hard at everybody. In this he may have been quite wrong; probably, perhaps he was so; but I am not convinced at all, but what most of us would have done the same.

Some say that, in the bitterness of that wrong and outrage, he slew a gentleman of the Court, whom he supposed to have borne a hand in the plundering of his fortunes. Others say that he bearded King Charles the First himself, in a manner beyond forgiveness. One thing, at any rate, is sure – Sir Ensor was attainted, and made a felon outlaw, through some violent deed ensuing upon his dispossession . . .

In great despair at last, he resolved to settle in some outlandish part, where none could be found to know him; and so, in an evil day for us, he came to the West of England. Not that our part of the world is at all outlandish, according to my view of it (for I never found a better one), but that it was known to be rugged and large, and desolate. And here, when he had discovered a place which seemed almost to be made for him, so withdrawn, so self-defended, and uneasy of access, some of the country-folk around brought him little offerings – a side of bacon, a keg of cider, hung mutton, or a brisket of venison; so that for a little while he was very honest. But when the newness of his coming began to wear away, and our good folk were apt to think, that even a gentleman ought

> to work, or pay other men for doing it, and many farmers were grown weary of manners without discourse to them, and all cried out to one another, how unfair it was that owning such a fertile valley, young men would not spade or plough by reason of noble lineage – then the young Doones, growing up, took things they would not ask for . . .
>
> Perhaps their den might well have been stormed, and themselves driven out of the forest, if honest people had only agreed to begin with them at once, when first they took to plundering. But having respect for their good birth, and pity for their misfortunes, and perhaps a little admiration at the justice of God, that robbed men now were robbers, the squires and farmers, and shepherds, at first did nothing more than grumble gently, or even make a laugh of it, each in the case of others. After a while they found the matter gone too far for laughter, as violence and deadly outrage stained the hand of robbery, until every woman clutched her child, and every man turned pale at the very name of 'Doone'.

This Scottish background, so deftly fashioned by Blackmore, was regarded during his lifetime as a beguiling flight of fancy, a justifiable slice of romanticism suggestive of Sir Walter Scott. Yet, less than two years after his death, it received dramatic and compelling support.

On 12 October 1901 there appeared in the *West Somerset Free Press* an article entitled 'A Short History of the Original Doones of Exmoor: Their Descent and Reason of Their Exile'. This was written by Ida Marie Browne, who lived in Cambridge and employed the pen name 'Audrie Doon' to declare her kinship. It begins:

> Since my first visit to the West of England in 1899, it has occurred to me that it would be of no little interest to those visiting the neighbourhood to have some idea as to who were, in reality, the original outlaws mentioned in Blackmore's charming romance, and it seemed that I, a member of the Scotch family from which they sprang, should be the one to write it. It occasioned me no small surprise, on perusing *Lorna Doone* for the first time, to find its author had embodied the traditions of my progenitors so correctly, and I was still further surprised and interested to discover on visiting the haunts of my ancestors, that the story of the Doone family was one of the best known legends of the locality.

She then proceeds to give the history of the Doones. Sir Ensor Doone, her great-great-great-great-great-grandfather, was actually Ensor James Stewart, whose father was the twin of the second Earl of Moray, the 'bonny Earl' of ballad fame. The twins became enemies, and their sons continued the family feud. In 1618 Ensor defiantly took the surname Doune (as it was at that time),manifesting his right to Doune Castle, which had passed to the third Earl. This so enraged his cousin that he summoned sixteen of his clansmen, rode to Stirling and attacked and imprisoned Ensor in his own home. He offered him the alternatives of permanent confinement in Doune Castle or exile. Ensor chose the latter and, with his wife and one retainer, travelled straight to London, hoping to obtain redress from James I; but this was not forthcoming. 'Sir Ensor, disgusted with mankind in general, thereupon resolved to shut himself away from the world in the most remote district they could discover, and, at the end of a long and toilsome march of thirteen days, they found themselves on the bare plains of Exmoor.' Ensor died on Exmoor in 1684 at the age of 87. In August 1699 the Doones returned to Scotland, on the invitation of the fifth Earl of Moray, who wished to bring to an end the years of enmity.

After Audrie Doon's lengthy narrative, there are reproduced some genealogical notes made by her great-great-grandfather, Charles Doune. She also quotes from a journal kept by Rupert Doune, who visited Exmoor and noted on 3 September 1747, 'Got to Oare, and then to the valley of the Lyn, the scenery very bonny, like our own land, but the part extremely wild and lonely. Wandered about and thought of the old days, and of the doings of the family while here, which I gather were not peaceable.' In addition, she mentions the existence of certain mementos and relics, including a painting of Sir Ensor executed in 1679, a pair of bellows, a pistol on which are scratched 'C.Doone 1681' and 'Porlok', and a bootjack. Most of these were in the possession of

The East Lyn River, just north of Exmoor. The countryside here inspired not only the author of Lorna Doone, *but Coleridge, Wordsworth and Shelley before him.*

Audrie Doon's uncle, John William Beeton, an auctioneer, valuer and antique dealer. They were lost in a fire that destroyed his shop and studio in Hunstanton, Norfolk, on Sunday, 7 December 1902. None of the relics or documents to which Audrie Doon alluded is at present known to exist. However, photographs of the portrait and the pistol appeared in *The King* on 11 October 1902.

What are we to make of Audrie Doon and her article? Why has no other member of the Doone family, before or since, come forward to present corroborating evidence? What are we to make of John William Beeton and the relics that went up in smoke? Much of her article also disappears into thin air; we have no means of verifying it. We are left, too, with a sense of unease over the idiom of Rupert Doune's 1747 journal and the notes written by Charles Doune in 1804. Something we can check, though, is the information about the early years of Ensor Doone. We can examine Robert Douglas's *The Peerage of Scotland*, the validated Cotton manuscripts in the British Museum and John Philipot's 1660 catalogue of knights; we can search the archives of the College of Arms in London and the Lyon Office in Edinburgh. But the only conclusion we can reach is that Sir Ensor Doone never existed.

Naturally, this does not mean that the Doones never existed; it does not stop them being Scottish. And, in light of certain other theories, it does not stop them being practically anything else – even Welsh. In a letter to *The Athenaeum* on 9 September 1905, Owen Rhoscomyl wrote:

> The clan of the Doones, and a famous clan at that, lived no further away than the other shore of the Bristol Channel, on the coast of Carmarthen, where the clan was famous as turbulent even in that land of turbulence. Not only the Doones lived there, but they lived there cheek by jowl with the Ryds of the same neighbourhood, and even intermarried with them on occasions. Moreover, one distinct feature of this clan was that it seemed to claim, as part of its inheritance, the right to burn the towns of Carmarthen and Kidwelly, and to kill the mayors. For these performances certain members of the clan regularly disappeared from the pedigree with the entry against their name 'fled to England', or 'left the country'. Of course, the Welsh way of spelling the name is 'Dwn', pronounced 'Doon'. They were descendants in the male line of the old princes of the country, and the pedigree of the chief branches of them may be found at large in the volume of pedigrees collected by the Elizabethan Herald, Lewis Dwn.
>
> The other piece of evidence is that Blackmore wrote a book called 'The Maid of Sker' [1872], to collect the evidence for which he must have gone very close to the Doon country, and would, therefore, be quite likely to learn something of the old Doons and Ryds.

It has been suggested, as well, that over the centuries the Doones became confused with the Danes, who raided the Somerset and Devon coasts during the Middle Ages. The Danes undoubtedly made a lasting impact on the area. Dousborough Hill is known also as Danesborough Hill; the Valley of Rocks is sometimes called Danes' Combe or The Danes. William Wordsworth's poem *The Danish Boy* (1799) was inspired by a visit to the Quantocks. Some believe the Doone legends to be no more than blurred souvenirs from those distant times when Viking hordes plundered on Exmoor. (Is it by chance that *Ensor* is an anagram of *Norse*?)

A further hypothesis pictures the Doones as soldiers who, having suffered defeat in either the Civil War or the Battle of Sedgemoor, escaped to Exmoor and became bandits. But all these speculations must ultimately confront the fact that none of the leading Exmoor historians has discovered a single reference to them. Collinson's *The History and Antiquities of the County of Somerset* (1791), Warner's *A Walk through the Western Counties* (1799), Williams's *A Tour in North Devon* (1802), Rawle's *Annals of the Ancient Forest of Exmoor* (1893), Chadwyck Healey's *The History of Part of West Somerset* (1901) and MacDermot's *A History of the Forest of Exmoor* (1911) all draw a blank. Dealing with the period 1653–96, when James Boevey was owner of Exmoor, MacDermot writes:

> It is during Boevey's tenancy of Exmoor Forest, covering as it did practically all the second half of the seventeenth century, that the 'Doones', a legendary band of robbers, are thought by some to have been established in Badgworthy . . . From what we know of Mr Boevey, his constant lawsuits and frequent appeals to the law officers of the Crown, it is, to say the least, highly improbable that he would have tolerated for any length of time the existence on his borders of any such nest of thieves, who would certainly have made frequent raids on the forest sheep and cattle. Although the forester was not responsible for the safety of the beasts agisted there, any considerable amount of sheep stealing would of course have deterred farmers from sending their flocks to the moor and so have lessened his profits, a state of things which Mr James Boevey would have been the last man to suffer.

We are led to conclude that, if the Doones existed, their crimes must probably have been committed on a small scale within a restricted locality during a brief period.

Interest in both the robber family and Blackmore's romance has lost nothing of its fervour over more than a century. An outcome of this continuing enthusiasm was the founding in 1983 of the Lorna Doone Society, with Sir Atholl Oakeley as its president. How many other novels have received such an accolade (and at so venerable an age)? One of the Society's most urgent objectives is to solve the mystery of the Doones. Its members believe themselves to be on the brink of unearthing proof that Sir Ensor Doone was a real person, that he left Scotland after a family dispute and settled on Exmoor. They regard Audrie Doon's evidence as correct in all save a few details; her single major error was to infer from a particular document that Sir Ensor's father was the twin of the 'bonny Earl' of Moray. He was, in fact, the cousin. Moreover, Ensor not only appropriated the name Doone, but also 'Enzie', which, being unfamiliar to Devonians, was converted during the course of time into the West Country name 'Ensor'; we may recollect that Carver Doone's little son was called Ensie. The Society's members are sure that most of the events in the novel actually took place a hundred years later and were moved back to the seventeenth century by Blackmore so he could introduce Monmouth's rebellion and the Battle of Sedgemoor. In their opinion, Tom Faggus lived in the eighteenth century and was similarly plucked out of his time. As Audrie Doon stated, the family returned to Scotland, including Carver Doone, who did not perish in the Wizard's Slough. Surprisingly, the Society feels that the heroine's name was probably not Lorna Doone and that she may well have died after being shot by Carver in Oare Church.

There is a part of us that might want to smile at the investigations and conjectures of the Lorna Doone Society; but isn't there another part that would desperately like them to hit the jackpot?

John Ridd in combat with some of the Doones during their attack on his farm

4

Cruel Coppinger

We owe the story of Cruel Coppinger largely to Robert Stephen Hawker, the extraordinary vicar of Morwenstow who imprinted his personality so vividly on the northern tip of Cornwall, just below Hartland Point, that the surrounding area, with its dramatic rocky coastline, has come to be known as Hawker Country. Hawker was undeniably an eccentric, as Sabine Baring-Gould makes clear in his biography *The Vicar of Morwenstow* (1876).

> Mr Hawker, as has been already intimated, was rather peculiar in his dress. At first, soon after his induction to Morwenstow, he wore his cassock; but in time abandoned this inconvenient garb, in which he found it impossible to scramble about his cliffs. He then adopted a claret-coloured coat, with long tails. He had the greatest aversion to anything black: the only black things he could wear were his boots. These claret-coloured coats would button over the breast, but were generally worn open, displaying beneath a knitted blue fisherman's jersey. At his side, just where the Lord's side was pierced, a little red cross was woven in the jersey. He wore fishing-boots reaching above his knee. . . .
>
> At first he went about in a college cap; but after speedily made way for a pink or plum-coloured beaver hat without a brim, the colour of which rapidly faded to a tint of pink, the blue having disappeared. When he put on coat, jersey or hat he wore it till it was worn out: he had no best suit. . . .
>
> He was usually followed to church by nine or ten cats, which entered the chancel with him and careered about it during service. . . Originally ten cats accompanied him to church, but one, having caught, killed and eaten a mouse on a Sunday, was excommunicated, and from that day was not allowed again within the sanctuary.

It has been suggested that Hawker's account of Cruel Coppinger proceeded from his lively imagination, not from meticulous research. Yet he was a man of unswerving honesty and integrity, whose nature it was to write flamboyantly and poetically because he was flamboyant and a poet. He won the

Newdigate Prize for poetry at Oxford in 1827; he was praised by Sir Walter Scott; Charles Dickens, as editor of *Household Words* and *All the Year Round,* published several of his works.

Hawker's first mention of Coppinger is in 'The Remembrances of a Cornish Vicar', which appeared in *All the Year Round* on 11 March 1865, when he was 61. He relates that a hoary parishioner told him:

> 'There was one Coppinger cast ashore from a brig that struck up at Hartland, on the Point. Farmer Hamlyn dragged him out of the water and took him home, and was very kind to him. Lord, sir, he never would leave the house again. He lived upon the folks a whole year, and at last, lo and behold! he married the farmer's daughter Elizabeth, and spent all her fortin rollicking and racketing, till at last he would tie her to the bedpost and flog her till her father would come down with more money. The old man used to say he wished he'd let Coppinger lie where he was in the waves, and never laid a finger on him to save his life. Ay, and divers more I've heerd of that never brought no good to they that saved them.'

Writing to his brother-in-law John Somers James, eighteen months later, on 25 September 1866, Hawker asked, 'Do you remember Bold Coppinger the Marsland Pirate? He died 87 years ago. I am collecting materials for his life for *All the Year Round.* If you know any anecdotes of him or Dinah his wife, will you let me know.' *Cruel Coppinger* was published in the magazine on 15 December 1866 and was included, four years afterwards, in Hawker's book *Footprints of Former Men in Far Cornwall.* In this article, he quotes the first stanza of an old ballad:

> Will you hear of the Cruel Coppinger?
> He came from a foreign kind:
> He was brought to us by the salt water,
> He was carried away by the wind.

Contrary to what the old man said about Coppinger being rescued from the sea, Hawker by then believed he came ashore without assistance, in the middle of a hurricane.

He was sighted by people watching for wreck while the boat he was skippering contended with mountainous seas; one could distinguish him from the rest of the crew by his massive size. Losing its battle with the tempest, the boat would clearly not reach safety. Coppinger stripped off his clothes and plunged into the churning surf. For several seconds, he disappeared from view, then he could be seen buffeting the breakers, his mighty shoulders and arms propelling him through the white-capped waves. With powerful, untiring strokes, he threshed a path towards the shore. Suddenly, a huge retreating roller wheeled back into the ocean, and he was standing on the beach, as sand and shingle, hissing and rattling, streamed past his ankles. A large crowd had gathered, on foot and on horseback. He strode into their midst, twitched a red cloak from a woman's back and flung it round him. He made his way towards an attractive girl sitting on a fine horse, jumped up behind her, grasped the bridle and kicked in his heels. The animal sped off, galloping homewards. When they reached her father's house he dismounted, swung down the girl, whose name was Dinah Hamlyn, and rapped on the door. He was given food and lodging and invited to stay until he had recovered from his ordeal.

He decided to stay indefinitely, making himself completely at home and, before too long, winning Dinah's heart. He disclosed that he came from a wealthy Danish family of high standing; he went to sea to avoid a marriage with a titled woman that his parents had arranged. Mr and Mrs Hamlyn were charmed by their guest and delighted at the attentions he paid their daughter. After he had been with them some little while, Mr Hamlyn suffered an unforeseen illness that led abruptly to his death. Coppinger at once took over the role of head of the family, behaving as if it were obviously his unquestioned right, which Mrs Hamlyn, distracted by the loss of her husband, made no attempt to dispute. Shortly afterwards he and Dinah were married and he stamped his authority even more firmly on the running of the home. His true nature now began to assert itself and, having been held in check for so lengthy a period, broke out with alarming violence. The doors of the house were thrown open wide to every villain dwelling in the vicinity; the place became their den and refuge. In Hawker's words:

> All kinds of wild uproar and reckless revelry appalled the neighbourhood day and night. It was discovered that an organised band of desperadoes, smugglers, wreckers, and poachers, were embarked in a system of bold adventure, and that 'Cruel Coppinger' was their captain. In those days, and in that unknown and far-away region, the peaceable inhabitants were totally unprotected. There was not a single resident gentleman of property or weight in the entire district: and the clergyman, quite insulated from associates of his own standing, was cowed into silence and submission. No revenue officer durst exercise vigilance west of the Tamar; and to put an end to all such surveillance at once, it was well known that one of the 'Cruel' gang had chopped off a gauger's [officer's] head on the gunwale of a boat, and carried the body off to sea.
>
> Amid such scenes, Coppinger pursued his unlawful impulses without check or restraint. Strange vessels began to appear at regular intervals on the coast, and signals were duly flashed from the headlands to lead them into the safest creek or cove. If the ground-sea were too strong to allow them to run in, they anchored outside the surf, and boats prepared for that service were rowed or hauled to and fro, freighted with illegal spoil. Amongst these vessels, one, a full-rigged schooner, soon

Galsham Farm, near Hartland, which Cruel Coppinger made his home during the 1790s. His signature scratched on a windowpane survived intact until 1916.

> became ominously conspicuous. She bore the name of the Black Prince, and was the private property of the Dane, built to his own order in a dockyard of Denmark. She was for a long time the chief terror of the Cornish Channel. Once with Coppinger on board, when, under chase, she led a revenue cutter into an intricate channel near the Gull Rock [a mile north of Morwenstow], where, from knowledge of the bearings, the Black Prince escaped scathless, while the king's vessel perished with all on board. In those times, if any landsman became obnoxious to Coppinger's men, he was either seized by violence or by craft, and borne away, handcuffed, to the deck of the Black Prince; where, to save his life, he had to enrol himself, under fearful oaths, as one of the crew. In 1835, an old man of the age of ninety-seven related to the writer that, when a youth, he had been so abducted, and after two years' service had been ransomed by his friends with a large sum. 'And all,' said the old man, very simply, 'because I happened to see one man kill another, and they thought I should mention it.'

Coppinger became wealthy and powerful. On a certain occasion, when buying a farm whose fields reached clear to the sea, he presented himself at the solicitor's office attended by a retainer staggering beneath a load of bulging, clinking sacks. These were then brusquely poured out across the desk, which overflowed with a deluge of gold and silver, with ducats, dollars, doubloons, sovereigns, kroner, louis d'or, pieces of eight, florins, guilders – the coinage of more than a dozen nations. The solicitor protested at this method of payment until Coppinger fixed him with his eye and told him to take it or leave it. Apart from acquiring much property and land, he held sway, too, over vast stretches of the countryside; men could come and go only in accordance with his decrees. He exercised exclusive control over particular pathways leading to the coast, and these became known as 'Coppinger's Tracks'. They converged at Steeple Brink, a headland near Morwenstow, where the cliff towered 300 feet above the beach. Within was an enormous cave – the size of the church of St James at nearby Kilkhampton – that could be entered only by a cable ladder suspended from the top of the cliffs; access was quite impossible from the beach. Here, Coppinger and his men brought all their spoil, which was stored in massive piles of iron-bound sea-chests, tubs, casks, boxes, crates, panniers, saddlebags, satchels, trunks and other containers. Here, too, they laid their plans, feasted and revelled.

Only one man sought to criticize Coppinger, and that was the rector of Kilkhampton. But he paid for his audacity.

> The clergyman had spoken above his breath of the evil doings in the cave and had thus aroused his wrath and vengeance. On a certain day he was jogging homeward on his parish cob, and had reached the middle of a wide and desolate heath. All at once he heard behind him the clattering of horse-hoofs and a yell such as might have burst from the throat of the visible demon when he hurled the battle on the ancient saint. It was Cruel Coppinger with his double-thonged whip, mounted on his terrible mare. Down came the fearful scourge on his victim's shuddering shoulders. Escape was impossible. The poor parson knew too well the difference between his own ambling galloway, that never essayed any swifter pace than a jog-trot, and that awful steed behind him with footsteps like the storm. Circling, doubling like a hare, twisting aside, crying aloud for mercy, all was vain. He arrived at last at his own house, striped like a zebra. . . .

Coppinger was not averse, either, to taking a cat-o'-nine-tails to his wife after strapping her upright and spread-eagled to the rough-hewn oak pillars of their bed. This was not pursued within the compass of an imaginative and comprehensive matrimonial relationship, but to terrify her mother into handing over more and more of the funds she inherited from her husband. Dinah may, of course, have been a willing party to this effective method of extortion. She and Coppinger had one child, a fine-looking boy with blond hair and flashing eyes, though, alas, he was deaf and dumb. Otherwise, he was a normal healthy boy, cruel to animals, sullen and uncouth. When he was six, so people maintained, he pushed another child to his death from the top of a cliff, for he was later found leaping up and down with delight while peering at the tiny twisted figure that lay far below on the sand. He would often return to the spot and, pointing to the beach, try to engage the attention of any passers-by.

Coppinger's fortunes eventually began to decline. It seems he became too ambitious, too reckless, and the forces of law and order paid him increasingly close attention. The time came for him to take leave of the West Country.

> His disappearance, like his arrival, was commemorated by a turbulent storm. A wrecker, who had gone to watch the shore, saw, as the sun went down, a full-rigged vessel standing off and on. By-and-by a rocket hissed up from the Gull Rock, a small islet with a creek on the landward side which had been the scene of many a run of smuggled cargo. A gun from the ship answered it, and again both signals were exchanged. At last a well-known and burly form stood on the topmost crag of the island rock. He waved his sword, and the light flashed back from the steel. A boat put off from the vessel, with two hands at every oar; for the tide runs with double violence through Harty Race. They neared the rocks, rode daringly through the surf, and were steered by some practised coxswain into the Gull Creek. There they found their man. Coppinger leaped on board the boat, and assumed the command. They made with strong efforts for their ship. It was a path of peril through that boiling surf. Still, bending at the oar like chained giants, the man watched them till they forced their way through the battling waters. Once, as they drew off the shore, one of the rowers either from ebbing strength or loss of courage, drooped at his oar. In a moment a cutlass gleamed over his head, and a fierce stern stroke cut him down. It was the last blow of Cruel Coppinger. He and his boat's crew boarded the vessel, and she was out of sight in a moment, like a spectre or a ghost.

This final scene was accompanied by thunder, lightning and hail. Trees were ripped from the ground by the violence of the gale. A fireball crashed through the roof of Coppinger's house and fell at the very foot of the chair in which he usually sat. Dinah held her son tightly and shook with fear.

As has been suggested earlier, we probably need not doubt the outline of Hawker's narrative. In *The Vicar of Morwenstow,* Baring-Gould confirms that he, too, has heard much the same tale from people in that part of the country. Nevertheless, there does seem to be a certain amount of embroidery, and a few points are perhaps worth mentioning. The story has similarities with the Cornish legend of the pirate-wrecker of Tregeseal, who, after coming ashore from a mystery vessel, pursued a life of monstrous crime. The unlikely episode of the gauger's head being chopped off on the gunwale had been previously used by Hawker in *The Gauger's Pocket* (1853). One of Hawker's envelope seals bore the word 'Thorough', which he states is Coppinger's motto. In his first draft of the article, the old ballad runs to two stanzas; in the published text, he says that only one stanza has survived.

No cliff near Morwenstow is called Steeple Brink; similarly, no cave in the area is the size of Kilkhampton Church, or even of much size at all. Coppinger's boat was the *Black Prince*, and this is the name of the boat, too, in Hawker's famous smuggling story *The Light of Other Days* (1853), which contains no allusion to Coppinger. It also happens to be the name of the boat used by Scotland's most famous smuggler, Yawkins, whom Scott turned into Dick Hatteraick in *Guy Mannering* (1815), to which novel Hawker refers in *The Gauger's Pocket.* A matter of interest, here, is that Yawkins was a Dutchman, which prompts us to remember that Coppinger was apparently a Dane. Hawker was drawn to Norse and Viking heroes, and a number of his poems are about them. Among the most moving moments in his life was when, after the wreck of the *Alonzo* near Morwenstow on 25 October 1843, he gazed upon the lifeless body of a young Danish sailor, Philip Bengstein, stretched on the beach, 'a fine and stately example of a man: he was six feet two inches in height, of firm and accurate proportion throughout; and he must have been, indeed, in life a shape of noble symmetry and grace' *(The Remembrances of a Cornish Vicar).* Hawker buried him in Morwenstow churchyard. Later, he heard from Bengstein's father, who 'told me in tearful words that his son had gone away from his native home because his parents had resisted a marriage which he was desirous to contract. They found that he had gone to sea before the mast, a position much below his station in life; and they had traced him from ship to ship, until at last they found him on the papers of the Alonzo, of Stockton-on-Tees.' We cannot help recall that Coppinger, as well, went to sea, though high-born, because of a disagreement with his parents over an intended marriage. Finally, there is a discrepancy between Hawker and Baring-Gould in regard to the time when Coppinger lived. Hawker, in the letter quoted above, implies that he died in 1779; in *Cruel Coppinger,* a man of ninety-seven relates that he was taken on board the *Black Prince* when a youth, that is to say, in about 1760. So, Hawker believed that he flourished a little after the middle of the eighteenth century. Baring-Gould, however, in *A Book of the West: Cornwall* (1899), not only provides fresh information, but suggests a later date. He says that, in addition to a house in Welcombe, 'Coppinger had a small estate at Roscoff, in Brittany, which was the headquarters of the smuggling trade during the European War. He was paid by the British Government to carry despatches to and from the French coast, but he took advantage of his credentials as a Government agent to do much contraband business himself.' This account brings Coppinger forward by thirty or forty years, placing him in the Napoleonic era.

Hawker loved to play hoaxes. He told people there were mermaids in the sea at Morwenstow, decked himself with seaweed and sat on a rock at the water's edge, combing his flowing locks and crooning in the moonlight. He also crept into the stable of the local doctor, trimmed his horse's mane and painted its body with black stripes, thus producing a highly plausible zebra, on which the unfortunate owner had to gallop through town in answer to a bogus call. Consequently, it could once have been surmised that *Cruel Coppinger,* with its numerous Hawker fingerprints, was another hoax. But several years after his death in 1875, some fascinating facts gradually came to light. A man named Daniel Herbert Coppinger had been wrecked at Welcombe Mouth on 23 December 1792 and given shelter by a farmer, William Arthur, who lived three miles north-eastward, in Goldenpark. On 3 August 1793, he was married in Hartland Parish Church to Anne Hamlyn, aged forty-two, whose parents' home was in Galsham, two miles south-west of Hartland. The register lists him as a member of the Royal Navy, though no record has been discovered to establish that he was in that service. He appears to have engaged in smuggling activities and stored his contraband in a cave at Sandhole Cliff, two miles south-west of Galsham. He was bankrupted and imprisoned in October 1802. He and his wife parted; she allegedly made him an allowance. She died a widow on 31 August 1833 in Barnstaple, where Coppinger himself is thought to have spent his later years.

Hawker was therefore correct on two important points: Coppinger *was* wrecked on the coast north of Morwenstow and he *did* marry a Miss Hamlyn. However, he may have been misled and confused, as was Baring-Gould, by the fact that there also existed a John Copinger, an outstandingly successful Roscoff merchant who supplied West Country smugglers with vast quantities of contraband. In tea alone, his company regularly achieved an annual turnover of around 400 000 lbs. His forebears came from Ireland, and three were outlawed for treason. Recently, it has been proposed that the family originated in Denmark and was named Copyner.

Despite all its inconsistencies, the legend of Cruel Coppinger endures. How much relates to Daniel Herbert Coppinger and how much to John Copinger and his family we may never know. In literature, Coppinger has inspired a number of works. By far the most popular is Baring-Gould's *In the Roar of the Sea,* which was printed in April 1892 and by 1969, when it appeared in paperback, had been reprinted seventeen times. In his introduction to William Purcell's biography of Baring-Gould, published in 1957, John Betjeman wrote:

> That novel *In the Roar of the Sea* about Polzeath, St Enodoc Church and Cruel Coppinger the smuggler, is still kept in print for the summer reading of visitors to the north coast of Cornwall, but it is dismissed by the sophisticated as romantic piffle. And I can remember my own faint doubts as to the authenticity of the tale when I first read it, for there was no cottage-like vicarage with roses round the door near St Enodoc and Pentine Glaze farm, which was pointed out to me as the home of Cruel Coppinger, did not seem to be as old or imposing as the novel had led me to expect. These errors did not detract from the story and I am sure that no one who starts to read *In the Roar of the Sea* (by no means the best of Baring-Gould's novels) will put it down unfinished, for it has that quality of all his novels, remarkable narrative-power.

5

The Gubbins

The Gubbins were a tribe of savages who for two centuries terrorized the area of Devon that lies around the Lyd Valley. Known variously as Gubbins, Gubbinses, Gybbins and Gubbings, they lived in makeshift huts or in the nooks and crannies of Lydford Gorge. Members of the clan first settled there during the fifteenth century; by the time of Charles I their numbers had swollen to several hundreds. They spurned marriage, but were otherwise domestically conventional, engaging in promiscuity and incest.

Their stranglehold on the Brentor–Lydford region was apparently complete before the end of the sixteenth century. In Chapter 14 of *Westward Ho!* (1855), Charles Kingsley gives a vivid impression of the fear they struck into the hearts of travellers, as the novel's heroes, Amyas Leigh and Salvation Yeo, set out for Bideford from the south coast during the autumn of 1583.

> . . . it was by no means a safe thing in those days to travel from Plymouth to the north of Devon; because, to get to your journey's end, unless you were minded to make a circuit of many miles, you must needs pass through the territory of a foreign and hostile potentate, who had many times ravaged the dominions and defeated the forces of her Majesty Queen Elizabeth, and was named (behind his back at least) the King of the Gubbings . . . Amyas, in fear of these same Scythians and heathens, rode out of Plymouth on a right good horse, in his full suit of armour, carrying lance and sword, and over and above two great dags, or horse-pistols; and behind him Salvation Yeo, and five or six north Devon men (who had served with him in Ireland, and were returning on furlough), clad in head-pieces and quilted jerkins, each man with his pike and sword, and Yeo with arquebuse and match, while two sumpter ponies carried the baggage of this formidable troop.
>
> They pushed on as fast as they could, through Tavistock, to reach before nightfall Lydford, where they meant to sleep; but what with buying the horses, and other delays, they had not been able to start before noon; and night fell just as they reached the frontiers of the enemy's country. A dreary place enough it was, by the wild glare of sunset. A high table-land of heath, banked on the right by the crags and hills of

> Dartmoor, and sloping away to the south and west toward the foot of the great cone of Brent-Tor, which towered up like an extinct volcano (as some say that it really is), crowned with the tiny church, the votive offering of some Plymouth merchant of old times, who vowed in sore distress to build a church to the Blessed Virgin on the first point of English land which he should see. Far away, down those waste slopes, they could see the tiny threads of blue smoke rising from the dens of the Gubbings; and more than once they called a halt, to examine whether distant furze-bushes and ponies might not be the patrols of an advancing army. It is all very well to laugh at it now, in the nineteenth century, but it was no laughing matter then; as they found before they had gone two miles farther.

Kingsley's stalwarts are then attacked by a dozen of the savages. However, Salvation Yeo not only dispatches them almost single-handed, without injury to himself – "Not a scratch, thank Heaven!" – but, for good measure, also kills the King of the Gubbings.

We do not know whether the Gubbins were ever actually ruled by a king, though Stanzas 10 and 11 of William Browne's poem *Lydford Journey*, dating from around 1620–30, certainly suggest they had a leader.

> And near hereto's the Gubbins' cave;
> A people that no knowledge have
> Of law, or God, or men:
> Whom Caesar never yet subdued;
> Who've lawless liv'd; of manners rude;
> All savage in their den.
>
> By whom, – if any pass that way,
> He dares not the least time to stay,
> For presently they howl;
> Upon which signal they do muster
> Their naked forces in a cluster,
> Led forth by Roger Rowle.

Rowle's Pool, near the Devil's Cauldron in Lydford Gorge, commemorates the man who evidently commanded the Gubbins at some stage during the first half of the seventeenth century. He also appears in Anna Eliza Bray's novel *Warleigh* (1830), set in the days of the Civil War. Here he takes on an epic, legendary stature, as we can see from Chapter 25.

> . . . for Roger Rowle, as lawless as he was brave, was the Robin Hood of Devon in the times of Charles the First . . . however lawless might now be the life of this extraordinary person, he had once gallantly served as a volunteer in the king's cause, and had shown, in the midst of many

Brentor and its dramatically sited church, near Lydford, home of the heathen Gubbins. According to legend, the church's construction was prolonged by the Devil's interference.

> wild and desperate acts, a generosity and spirit of self-devotion that made his afterlife to be regretted, if not pitied, by all who honoured loyalty and courage.

Two chapters later, Mrs Bray sheds a similar lustre on the Gubbins.

> Though the followers of Roger Rowle, at the time we introduce them to the reader, assuredly deserved no other name than that of banditti, yet, in the first instance, they were not altogether unworthy of pity – since injustice, cruelty, and persecution, had driven them into distress; and afterwards, rendered desperate by the want of that mercy which, if timely shown, might have reclaimed them, they became confirmed in their errors till, totally hardened by repeated acts of violence and aggression, they were both hunted and dreaded by all the country around . . . One of their family had been a dealer in cattle, and his trade was so considerable that, during some years of industry, he had amassed a fortune sufficient to enable him not only to provide for his own offspring (who were in number seven sons and three daughters), but also to assist his poor kindred to the third and fourth degree, so that, like a Scotch clan, the Gubbinses of Devon were a combined and powerful family amongst the yeomanry of the county. They were all to a man devoted to the cause of King Charles, and some of them had served him in more than one action.

Their transition from loyalist squires to marauding outlaws, relates Mrs Bray, was the outcome of a chain of events that began with the seduction and betrayal of John Gubbins's seventeen-year-old daughter by an officer in the Royalist army. An appeal to the garrison commander, Sir Richard Grenville, resulted not in the officer's punishment, but in the imprisonment in Lydford Castle of several of the Gubbins on a fabricated charge. A daring attack led by Roger Rowle secured their release. Thereafter, the entire clan, abandoning home and hearth, was relentlessly pursued by Grenville's forces. Eventually, John Gubbins was captured and hanged. Rowle now embarked on bloody revenge, starting with the murder of the Gubbins girl's seducer. Soon, however, necessity compelled him to sanction widespread acts of robbery and plunder; the feud with Grenville was overshadowed by the struggle for survival.

Anna Eliza Bray's romantic treatment of the Gubbins contrasts strikingly with the description given by Thomas Fuller in *The History of the Worthies of England*, published in 1662, two years after the accession of Charles II.

> . . . the *Gubbings-Land* is a Scythia within England, and they pure Heathens therein. It lyeth nigh Brent-Tor, in the edg of Dartmore. It is reported, that, some *two hundred* years since, *two Strumpets* being with child, fled hither to hide themselves, to whom certain lewd Fellows resorted, and this was their first original. They are a *Peculiar* of their own making, exempt from *Bishop*, *Archdeacon*, and all Authority either *Ecclesiastical* or *Civil*. They live in *Cotts* (rather *Holes* than *Houses*) like *Swine*, having all in common, *multiplied* without *marriage* into many *hundreds*. Their language is the *drosse* of the *dregs* of the *vulgar Devonian*; and the more learned a man is, the worse he can understand them. During our Civil Wars, no Souldiers were *quartered* amongst them, for fear of being *quartered* amongst them. Their *wealth* consisteth in *other men's goods*, and they live by stealing the Sheep on the Moore; and vain it is for any to search their Houses, being a work *beneath* the pains of a *Sheriff*, and *above* the *power* of any Constable. Such their *fleetnesse*, they will outrun many *horses*; *vivaciousnesse*, they outlive *most men*; living in the ignorance of *luxury*, the *extinguisher* of life. They hold together like *Burrs*; offend *one*, and *all* will revenge his quarrel.
>
> But now I am informed, that they begin to be civilized, and tender their Children to Baptisme, and return to be men, yea Christians again. I hope no *Civil People* amongst us will turn Barbarians, now these Barbarians begin to be *civilized.*

Fuller suggests that the members of the tribe received their name as a term of abuse. In those days, gubbings were '*Sharings* of *Fish* (which are little worth)'; furthermore, 'the Word importeth *shame* and *disgrace*'. The modern meaning of 'gubbins' still implies insignificance, but no longer carries an

An engraving dated 1785 of Lydford Gorge, once the forbidding stronghold of the Gubbins; it is now a National Trust beauty spot

intimation of shame or disgrace. However, Fuller, who had no particular connection with Devon, may be wrong, and Mrs Bray, who lived in Tavistock for a quarter of a century, may be right in supposing that Gubbins was an actual surname. Concluding Chapter 27 of *Warleigh*, she mentions, 'The writer of these pages has been assured that within the last century several of their descendants (who still bore their uncouth name) lived near Brentor, and retained the rude and even savage character of their ancestors.' Documents surviving from eighteenth-century Lydford reveal that the population *did* include people called Gubbins. In 1745 and 1761 George Gubbins and Mary Gubbins were witnesses to leases, their rudeness and savagery apparently notwithstanding.

It seems that by the second half of the seventeenth century the Gubbins were in decline. This may have been exacerbated by the debilitating effects of chronic inbreeding and hastened, too, by their gradual conversion to Christianity. There is the possibility that, during the Commonwealth, Jesuit priests hid in Lydford Gorge to avoid Cromwell's forces.

Mrs Bray's *Traditions, Legends, Superstitions, and Sketches of Devonshire* (1838) paints a pathetic picture of the Gubbins in the nineteenth century.

> They still have the reputation of having been a wild and almost savage race; and not only this, but another name, that of *cramp-eaters*, is still applied to them by way of reproach.
>
> Instead of buns, which are usually eaten at country revels, in the West of England, the inhabitants of Brent Tor could produce nothing but cramps, an inferior species of cake; probably owing to the badness of their corn, from the poverty of the soil.

Those who once caused their neighbours' blood to freeze with fear are now pre-eminently associated with the production of low-grade buns.

A century later, according to Sabine Baring-Gould in *A Book of Dartmoor* (1900),

> It cannot be said that the race is altogether extinct. The magistrates have had much trouble with certain persons living in hovels on the outskirts of the moor, who subsist in the same manner. They carry off lambs and young horses before they are marked, and when it is difficult, not to say impossible, for the owners to identify them. Their own ewes always have doubles.

The Gubbins have thus virtually disappeared. Is Baring-Gould really writing about them, or about thieves who happened to follow in their footsteps on Dartmoor?

6

John Fitz

On the Plymouth Road in Tavistock, opposite the commanding statue of Sir Francis Drake, stands Fitzford Gate, all that remains of the Fitzford House estate, which once added much lustre to this handsome town. The Fitzes occupied Fitzford House for many generations, growing in wealth and influence, and reaching their zenith towards the end of the sixteenth century. During that period, in 1575, John Fitz was born, heir to the entire family fortune and properties, which were situated in Cornwall and Kent, as well as Devon. His father, who dabbled in astrology, cast the boy's horoscope immediately before his birth and, aghast at what the future seemed to hold, instructed the midwife to retard the delivery by an hour, but this proved impracticable. John belied these gloomy prognostications by developing into an attractive, sensible and intelligent youth. In 1590 his father died; there is a fine effigy of him in Tavistock parish church, with his young son kneeling beside him. John married shortly before attaining his majority. In 1596 his wife, Bridget, bore him a daughter whom they called Mary, and he came of age, succeeding to the Fitz riches. He now took over Fitzford House, his mother first moving to Walreddon, a villa three miles south of Tavistock, and later to Plymstock.

Fitz then proceeded to do what so many have done in his situation: he abandoned restraint and plunged into a life of profligacy, dissipation and exorbitance. At first, the influence of his wife tempered his prodigality, but gradually he succumbed to the blandishments of fawning retainers and other libertine bootlickers who had flocked to join his entourage, and, before too long, he became degenerate and corrupt. Although this made him many new acquaintances, it cost him his friends from earlier days. Among the last to stand by him was Nicholas Slanning, who came from Bickleigh, a dozen miles to the south. One summer's afternoon in 1599 they were dining in Tavistock together with various neighbours and companions when Fitz drunkenly boasted that he owned outright every single foot of all his farms and fields. Slanning responded by recollecting that there was actually a small parcel of land that he himself owned, but which he gladly allowed Fitz to use without payment. Stung by his reminder, Fitz called him a liar, bombarded him with obscene oaths and threatened to stab him. Slanning, a man of

Tavistock's Fitzford Gate is thought to be where John Fitz and four accomplices brutally murdered Nicholas Slanning on his way home to Bickleigh

Bedford Square, Tavistock; John Fitz terrorized this fair town for almost a decade at the end of the sixteenth century

courage, defended himself verbally with skill and gave indication, fingering a formidable dagger, that he was equally prepared to protect himself physically. The confrontation went no further; their friends intervened and arranged a fragile reconciliation in which nobody very much believed. Shortly afterwards, Slanning made his departure and set off for Bickleigh. He had scarcely travelled any distance when Fitz and four of his minions came galloping up behind him. He turned to meet them, asking what they wanted. Fitz replied that he intended revenging himself for the slur inflicted upon him. All five fell on Slanning with their swords. He fought heroically until receiving a powerful blow to the head. As he staggered under the impact, Fitz ran him through. It is said that this hideous deed was carried out in front of Fitzford Gate.

Slanning's murder provoked widespread sorrow and anger, for he was greatly liked and admired. Fitz, realizing the enormity of his crime and the unlikelihood of avoiding a death sentence, fled to France. Within six months his mother and his wife managed to procure a reprieve for him, so long as his behaviour remained upright thereafter. He returned to England at the end of 1599 and at once fell into his former ways; disregarding his wife's concern for him and her successful intercession, he also threw himself headlong into wenching and whoring. He received no word of warning from any quarter and, seemingly invulnerable to prosecution, became increasingly callous and depraved, following with impunity the dictates of his voracious desires.

On the accession of James I in 1603, Fitz was honoured with a knighthood, for no better reason than that he came from a prominent family, had influential relations and was wealthy, but principally because the king from across the border wished to win support among the shires. This accolade, so misguidedly bestowed, far from acting as a brake on his licentiousness, served only to spur him towards greater depths of depravity. Thus emboldened, he entered upon an ever-widening circle of vices, welcoming to his table the very dregs of society, whose comradeship he flaunted in public. Tavistock groaned beneath the weight of his outrages; men were assaulted and women molested, property was wrecked, the townsfolk lay sleepless until the early hours while Fitz and his mob racketed drunkenly through the streets. Worse still, another murder was committed, and again Fitz avoided prosecution.

But powerful forces were beginning to gather against him. His lechery had proliferated to such a degree that Fitzford House came to resemble a brothel, and, glutted in lust, he found no further need for his wife, whom he turned out of doors. Taking little Mary with her, she returned to the home of her father, Sir William Courtenay, who immediately started investigating the inroads that Fitz had made into Bridget's personal property. Simultaneously, Nicholas Slanning's two sons and daughter initiated legal proceedings in order to obtain compensation for the death of their father. Learning of these measures, Fitz, apparently for the first time, showed signs of uneasiness about his future, particularly since his conditional pardon had not yet been made absolute, even though he now had a title. Accordingly, in the summer of 1605, when he was thirty, he resolved to seek advice in London on how best to counter the charges being laid against him and to improve his position in the eyes of the law.

He thus rode out from Tavistock, with a footman in attendance. Journeying towards the capital, he became more and more apprehensive, and, since the trip took many days, he found ample opportunity to meditate on his corrupt existence and bleak prospects. Through dwelling on those matters most troubling to him, he gradually overturned the balance of his reason and fell prey to frightening fantasies. At night, racked by nightmares, drenched in sweat, jerking his head this way and that, he shrieked and roared in torment. During the day, crouching on his horse, lacerated by his own imagination, he would start in terror as mirages sprang towards him – phantoms of Sir William Courtenay or the dashing young Gamaliel Slanning spurring out of the distance at the head of many horsemen. The nearer he approached London, the more violent and chaotic became his agonized delusions, the more unhinged his mind.

Nearing his final destination, he found lodging late in the evening at a victualler's. His host, Daniel Alley, gave up his own bed for him, sending his wife into the children's room. Fitz, who now dreaded sleep but was equally afraid to lie awake with the spectres that haunted him, prevailed upon Alley to sit with him during the early hours. He dozed fitfully, tossing to and fro, his limbs writhing in anguish; every few minutes blood-curdling screams would burst from his foaming, twisted mouth. At about five o'clock, Alley, who had scarcely slept a wink, threw off his cloak and left the room to prepare for his day's work. While he was at the pump he heard a violent sound and, turning round, saw Fitz in his nightshirt coming at him with a rapier, his face contorted in a horrible grimace. Alley ran down the garden, with Fitz at his heels. He reached the garden gate, wrenched it open and was slamming it behind him, when Fitz, with manic force, drove his rapier straight through the timber and on through Alley's shoulder and chest, killing him almost at once.

Hearing his dying wail, Alley's wife rushed from her bed, out of the house and straight into the path of Fitz, who instantly levelled at her his blade, still dripping with her husband's blood. She fell on her knees, clasped her hands together and begged him to spare her life for the sake of her three children. Impervious to her pleas and now no longer in control of his movements, he twice struck at her and twice missed. Again he lunged and this time ripped through her nightdress, slicing into her arm. She keeled over, picked herself up and staggered into the house. He made no attempt to follow, but stood for several seconds immobile. Then, his brow at last unknotting, he strode purposefully to the garden wall, in which he firmly wedged the hilt of his rapier. He stepped a few paces backwards, paused for a moment and hurled himself against the point. It ran deep into his chest, jerking the weapon out of the wall. He dropped to the ground and, displaying prodigious power, pulled out the sword and flung it from him. The blood pumped from his wound, into which he slid his fingers to assure himself of its extent. But a quick death eluded him. 'Proud heart, wilt thou not yield?' he exclaimed, '. . . that I, thy owner, may not live, to hear the honour of my credit stained with these my odious acts!' He crawled to where his rapier lay, took it in hand, laboriously rose to his feet and lurched to the garden wall. Once more he anchored the hilt, once more backed away, once more thrust his breast onto its point. This time he impaled himself with such violence that the blade passed through his body and out of his back. And again, drawing on amazing reserves of strength, he dragged it inch by inch from his heaving chest, until the blood spurted unchecked. He swayed towards the door of the house and collapsed across the threshold, spouting like a stuck pig. Neighbours soon arrived and, after overcoming their horror and revulsion at the sight of Alley's corpse and of Fitz floundering in his own gore, they carried him upstairs and laid him on a bed. Some of them sped away to fetch medical help, while others did what they could to save his life. Before long the first doctor appeared. Fitz was given such skilled attention, particularly by the surgeon Quincy from Brentford, that, against all expectation, the flow of blood was successfully stanched and his wounds plugged. But, after the physicians had left, he cried out that he was determined to die and, frenziedly tearing away his bandages and dressings, compelled his life's blood to ebb afresh.

Meanwhile, the Earl of Northumberland, learning of Fitz's imminent demise, dispatched a chaplain from his residence at neighbouring Syon Park, across the river from Kew. The cleric exhorted the dying man to make a full confession and to repent his sins. He also tried to persuade him to accept medical assistance, to desist from taking his own life. But Fitz made little response to these entreaties, other than to speak of his regret at having murdered Daniel Alley; his principal concern was to bring his life to an end. The chaplain asked him whether he did not feel an obligation to provide for Alley's widow and three children. Fitz replied that he lamented having attacked her also and that, for all the wrong he had done her, he sought to atone with the donation of one hundred pounds. Despite being so near death, he was still panic-stricken that Sir William Courtenay would shortly catch up with him and blow him to pieces with explosives. His constitution must have been exceptionally robust, for two complete days elapsed before the self-inflicted injuries finally destroyed him.

Because of his rank in society, Fitz was granted the distinction of interment in the chancel of St Mary's, Twickenham, a stone's throw north of Eel Pie Island. He was laid to rest on 10 August 1605.

7

The Greggs

The earliest account of the Greggs was published in about 1770 in an eight-page chapbook entitled *The History of John Gregg, and His Family of Robbers and Murderers.* Before long the Greggs became known as the Cannibals of Clovelly; today, two centuries later, their story still makes gruesome reading.

The chapbook relates that John Gregg was born about eight or nine miles east of Exeter – presumably somewhere near Marsh Green. As a young man, he worked at hedging and ditching, 'but being very much adicted to Idleness, and not chusing to be confined to any honest Employment, he left his Father and Mother, and ran away into the desert part of the Country, taking with him a Woman, as viciously inclined as himself.' The two of them eventually arrived at Clovelly, where they made their home by the seashore in an underground cave that could be reached only through an immensely long, winding passageway. They lived there for the next quarter of a century, gathering about them a family of eight sons, six daughters and thirty-two grandchildren 'begotten by Incest'. They supported themselves by robbery, always murdering their victims, whom they carried off to their cave. The bodies were carefully cut up, the edible portions being either pickled or hung before cooking. The murders thus served two ends: the eradication of witnesses to the Greggs' crimes, and the provision of food.

The continual and numerous disappearances in the vicinity of Clovelly caused terror and bewilderment. 'This occasioned spies to be sent into these parts, many of whom never returned again, and those who did after the strictest search and enquiry could not find out how the melancholy matters happened.' Neighbour regarded neighbour with fearful distrust, and in an atmosphere of alarm and perplexity several members of the community were sent to the gallows. Quite a few visitors to the town met with the same fate. Those to suffer most were the innkeepers, who frequently attracted suspicion when their guests vanished; their ranks were reduced by hanging, by defection to less hazardous employment, or by departure to other regions. With less and less accommodation available to travellers, Clovelly became increasingly isolated, while the rapacity of the Greggs and the flustered over-zealousness of the law steadily contributed towards the town's depopulation.

Blackchurch Rock, near Clovelly, from an engraving of 1822; somewhere nearby the Greggs reputedly inhabited a cave in which they pickled and ate their victims

As the Greggs grew in number, their needs also increased, and at length they would descend on groups of as many as six people. During their twenty-five years in Clovelly they were responsible for about a thousand deaths. Their downfall came as the result of an attack on a husband and wife riding home on their horse one evening from a fair. The man fought bravely, defending himself well, but the woman was brought off the horse and instantly murdered, 'the female cannibals cutting her throat, and sucking her blood with as great gust as tho' it had been Wine. This done, they ripp'd her up, and pull'd out her Entrails. . . .' Her husband, crazed with grief, now laid furiously about him, putting up astonishing resistance and, before he could be taken, a crowd of some thirty people, also returning from the fair, suddenly came into view. The Greggs, much outnumbered, had no alternative but to abandon the man and run off through the nearby woods. The man, the first ever to have survived an encounter with the Greggs, told everyone what had happened and showed them the remains of his wife. His melancholy tale was received in stunned and barely comprehending silence.

A deputation immediately journeyed to Exeter and told the mayor of this latest episode. He, in turn, sent word to the king, who shortly afterwards set out with about 400 soldiers. In Clovelly, the king, bent on finally ridding his realm of such monstrous criminals, spared no pains in trying to locate them. The soldiers used bloodhounds and it was these animals who, after several days' search, at last discovered the entrance to the Greggs' cave, which the soldiers had earlier disregarded. When the king came along the shore and inspected the entrance he was doubtful whether it could lead anywhere, but the hounds were so aroused that he gave the order to press forward.

> Torches were immediately had, and a great many Men enter'd thro' the most intricate Windings, 'till they came to the private Recess of the Murderers: then the whole Body of them went in, and saw the dismal sight and were ready to sink into the earth to see such a Multitude of Arms, Legs, Thighs, Hands and Feet, of Men, Women and Children hung up in Rows, like dry'd Beef and a great many lying in Pickle. They also found a Quantity of Money, Watches, Rings, Swords, Pistols and a large Quantity of Cloathes and other Things, which they had taken from those they had murdered.

By a stroke of good fortune the entire Gregg family was present, and they were seized and taken to Exeter. The human remains found in the cave were buried in the sand.

After passing a day in prison in Exeter, the Greggs were removed to Plymouth for execution. The usual legal processes were denied them, because of their manifest guilt and the enormity of their crimes. The adult male Greggs were executed by a procedure that seems to have been unashamedly imitative of their own methods. 'The Men had first their Privy Members cut off and thrown into the Fire before their Faces; and then their Hands and Legs were cut off, by which Amputation they bled to death some Hours afterwards.' The women and children, having witnessed these assorted dismemberments, were burnt to death, heaped up in three separate fires. None of the Greggs showed the least sign of repentance; indeed, they cursed and swore 'the most horrid Imprecations to the last Gasp of Breath'.

The great drawback to this grisly and engrossing chronicle is that it seems to be spurious. An earlier account, which is practically identical, word for word, but has the story taking place on the Galloway coast in Scotland during the reign of Elizabeth I, appears in Captain Charles Johnson's *A General and True History of the Lives and Actions of the Most Famous Highwaymen, Murderers, Street-Robbers, etc.*, published in London in 1734. Captain Charles Johnson was a pseudonym of Daniel Defoe; a similar Defoe volume, *A General History of the Robberies and Murders of the Most Notorious Pyrates* (1724), has Johnson as author. However, since Defoe died in April 1731, the *General and True History* of 1734 was obviously produced by someone who realized the advantage of perpetuating a successful name. In this book, the leader of the cannibals is called Sawney Beane. He was born about eight or nine miles east of Edinburgh and, after working at hedging and ditching, ran away with a woman to the Galloway coast. Following his arrest twenty-five years later, he was taken to Edinburgh and thence to Leith, where he was executed, together with the other members of his family. Several Sawney Beane chapbooks were printed towards the end of the eighteenth century and, like the John Gregg chapbook, they ran to eight pages, in the form of a broadsheet with four pages on either side. This was a highly economical method of publication and the usual cover price was one penny. Purchasers nevertheless expected value for money, with all eight pages filled. As far as the John Gregg/Sawney Beane chapbooks were concerned, the problem lay not in providing sufficient text, but in satisfactorily reducing the narrative in Johnson's *General and True History.* It is interesting that all the chapbooks – maybe it was a matter of follow-my-leader – chose to omit the following passage:

> And, notwithstanding, they were at last so numerous, they commonly had Superfluity of this their abominable Food; so that in the Night-time they frequently threw Legs, and Arms of the unhappy Wretches they had murdered, into the Sea, at a great Distance from their bloody Habitation. The Limbs were often cast up by the Tide in several Parts of the Country, to the Astonishment and Terror of all the Beholders, and others who heard of it. Persons who have gone about their lawful Occasions fell so often into their Hands, that it caused a general Out-cry in the Country round about, no Man knowing what was become of his Friend or Relation if they were once seen by these merciless Cannibals.

The reason for leaving it out was perhaps because it came early on and the printer was anxious to start cutting as soon as possible; it is certainly not vital to the plot, neither does it wholly accord with the rest of the text.

The suggestion has been made that, somehow or other, John Gregg came before Sawney Beane, and that Sawney Beane is bogus, not John Gregg. But there can be no doubt that Johnson's Sawney Beane precedes by several decades anything else in print relating to the same story. We can see that other versions derive from Johnson by comparing extracts like the following:

> The Place where they inhabited was quite solitary and lonesome; and when the Tide came up, the Water went for near two hundred Yards into their subterraneous Habitation, which reached almost a Mile under Ground. . . . (Johnson, 1734)

> The Place they inhabited was solitary and lonesom, and when the Tide came up, it reached a Mile under Ground. . . . (John Gregg chapbook, c. 1770)

> The place they inhabited was solitary and lonesome; and when the tide came up, it went near two Hundred miles[!] under ground. . . . (Sawney Beane chapbook, c. 1795)

It could still be proposed that John Gregg might have come first in the oral tradition; but for what good reason would the *General and True History,* which was printed and published in Birmingham and London, turn him into Sawney Beane and transfer him from Clovelly to Galloway? There is every reason, though, why a printer in, say, Bristol or Yeovil, should decide to make himself some money by moving the story nearer home.

Another point to which we should perhaps turn our attention is the place of execution in the two separate stories. Sawney Beane was imprisoned in Edinburgh (though he could not have been put in the Tolbooth, as Johnson states) and executed in Leith. This presumably means Leith Walk, passing from Edinburgh into Leith, to which Robert Chambers refers in *The Traditions of Edinburgh* (1824). 'One terrible peculiarity attended Leith Walk in its former condition. It was overhung by a gibbet, from which were suspended all culprits whose bodies at condemnation were sentenced to be hung in chains. The place where this gibbet stood, called the Gallow Lee, is now a good deal altered in appearance.' The highwayman and incendiary Gilder Roy was chained forty feet above the ground when he met his end there in 1656. In contrast, the idea of imprisoning John Gregg and his family in Exeter and then marching them forty-five miles to Plymouth for execution is implausible. This was not the practice: execution would usually have taken place either in Exeter itself or, more probably, a mile out of the city at Heavitree Gallows, where, as late as 1782, a fifteen-year-old servant girl was burnt to death for poisoning her master. Plymouth formerly had little administrative or legislative importance, and criminals were customarily sent from that city to Exeter, not in the opposite direction. After the notorious Eulalia Page had supposedly dispatched her husband in Plymouth in 1591, she was sent for trial, and subsequent burning, as far away as Barnstaple, 'the plague being much at Exeter'. The explanation for the strange introduction of Plymouth in the John Gregg version appears to be the printer's poor choice of an alternative to Leith. To substitute Exeter for Edinburgh presented him with little difficulty, but, lacking local knowledge and perhaps using a limited map, he may have seen Plymouth as the only possibility, particularly since sending the cannibals up to Barnstaple would have meant returning them almost to their own doorstep.

It can also be remarked that no other source material mentions the Greggs. The village of Clovelly has no memory of their existence. Charles Kingsley, four of whose teenage years were spent there, does not include the Greggs in *Westward Ho!* (1855), which is partly set in Clovelly during the later years of Elizabeth I. He had an exceptional knowledge of the village, whose churchyard, J.L.W. Page observes in *The Coasts of Devon and Lundy Island* (1895), 'is to us like a chapter of Romance. Half the names we know in "Westward Ho!" are on its stones.' Yet in that novel Kingsley sends his muscular Christian heroes thirty miles south to Lydford for no better purpose than to beat up the Gubbins. If he wanted to biff heathen tribes, then why not the Greggs, who were chomping away practically within earshot?

8

Isaac Gulliver

Isaac Gulliver was described in a 1788 Board of Customs report as 'one of the greatest and most notorious smugglers in the West of England'. He was unquestionably the most prosperous, but it seems doubtful whether he ever achieved much notoriety, since he neither harmed nor cheated anybody. Indeed, he was not only generally liked, he was also admired for his commercial success. The same Board of Customs report admitted that 'He is a person of great speculating genius and besides the smuggling he has carried on a variety of other business.'

He was born in Semington, near Trowbridge, Wiltshire, on 5 September 1745. During his teens he served at sea and spent more than a year in Newfoundland, where fishing fleets from Poole were reaping a rich harvest. On 5 October 1768, when he was twenty-three, he married the daughter of the landlord of The Blacksmith's Arms, on the Salisbury–Blandford Forum road at Sixpenny Handley. Soon afterwards he took charge of the inn, altering its name to The King's Arms; the building still stands and is today called Old Thorney Down. By this time he was already making headway with his smuggling ventures, which were conducted along the stretch of coast running from Poole, through Bournemouth and Christchurch, to Highcliffe. Bournemouth, known as Bourne Heath, was six miles of desolate countryside with virtually no inhabitants; its development did not begin until the 1820s.

Gulliver's contemporaries were impressed by his imposing physique, his bravery and his powerful presence. He was highly intelligent, an instinctive leader and a gifted organizer. Before long he had more than a score of employees and was earning sufficient money not only to fund his own numerous enterprises, but to acquire property and make investments. In 1776 he purchased North Eggardon Farm on Eggardon Hill, five miles north-east of Bridport. At more than 800 feet above sea level, the land here provides outstanding views of Lyme Bay. Gulliver planted a large circle of firs to act as a seamark, but this was eventually destroyed – by excisemen, it is said. The immediate coast provided a number of landing sites used by Gulliver's men, including West Bay, Burton Bradstock, West Bexington and Abbotsbury. In 1777 he was doing well enough to be able to lend a farmer in Melbury Abbas £300 at 4½ per cent interest. In 1778 he relinquished his holding in The

Old Thorney Down, at Sixpenny Handley, formerly The King's Arms where Isaac Gulliver was landlord during the early days of his smuggling career

King's Arms and purchased The White Hart at Longham, directly north of Bournemouth and about five miles from the coast. This inn was ideally placed, a dozen miles nearer to his main sphere of operations. In 1780 he took possession of West Howe Lodge, Brook Road, Kinson, a mile south of Longham. He is believed to have had the house built to his own specifications. Unfortunately it was demolished in 1958, when the site was incorporated in a housing estate. In the dining-room floor was a trapdoor that led into an enormous cellar, issuing from which was an expertly constructed brick tunnel, about six feet high. We do not know how far this originally travelled, because in modern times it was sealed off about 40 feet from the entrance. Its continuation was probably lost at some stage during Kinson's evolution. Rather more intriguing was a secret room, in the middle of the house, that could be entered only through a concealed door half-way up the chimney.

In May 1782 the government offered a general pardon to any smuggler who expressed his willingness either to serve in the Royal Navy or to provide two suitable substitutes. Gulliver accepted the pardon; the substitutes would have presented no problem to a man of his resourcefulness. Nevertheless, he continued to organize smuggling activities that took place not only along most of the Dorset coast, but extended some distance into Hampshire and Devon. He used the Bourne Heath area more than any other, landing goods at points like Alum, Flag, Canford Cliffs and Branksome Chine. As his men travelled inland, they established paths that, half a century later, formed the basis of Bournemouth's burgeoning road network. Their booty consisted primarily of spirits and tea, although, from the mid-1780s onwards, the latter became less worthwhile owing to William Pitt's sweeping reductions in duty levels. Other items included wine, tobacco, playing cards, silk, lace, linen and snuff. In 1783 Gulliver announced himself to be a wine merchant. Somewhat surprisingly, this preposterous declaration appears to have convinced customs officials. The 1788 report, cited earlier, asserts that, after availing himself of the pardon, Gulliver 'afterwards confined himself chiefly to the wine trade which he carried on to a considerable extent having vaults at various places along the coast to the westwards of this port some of which it is said were situated in remote places and we are well informed that he constantly sold wines considerable under the fair dealers price from which circumstances there is no doubt but that he illicitly imported that article but which trade we are informed he dropped some time since.'

At the height of his career Gulliver employed about fifty or more men, whom he treated with a generosity and consideration that were unusual for the time. He gave them special clothing, a sort of livery, which was distinctive and smart, as well as saving them money. This consisted principally of a handsome smock, similar to that worn by Dorset shepherds. He encouraged them to grow their hair long, which they tied in a tail and powdered white. The powder, which Gulliver himself may have brought into the country, usually carried a high customs tax. To present his men to the world in such elegance and so recognizably was a roguish act of bravado that testified to his wealth and self-assurance. His own attire, though expensive and fashionable, was always in excellent taste. Very occasionally, and only when it was vital, he would wear a disguise, donning one of his men's outfits or assuming the rustic simplicity of a herdsman.

Gulliver continued to invest in property. In 1789, he bought what is now known as Gulliver's Farm in West Moors, seven miles north of Bournemouth. Soon afterwards he gained possession of a house with land at Long Crichel, six miles north-east of Blandford Forum. He also bought the imposing High House in Wimbourne Road, Corfe Mullen, and further property and land in Wimbourne Minster, Bourne Bottom, Dudsbury, near Longham, and West Howe, near Kinson. In addition, he owned a small fleet of ships, mostly schooners and luggers. We know disappointingly little about these vessels; no more than two, the schooner *Marieanne* and the lugger *The Dolphin*, have so far been identified.

Gulliver retired from smuggling shortly before he was sixty, during the first decade of the nineteenth century. His final run, involving every man in his employ, was spectacular. His three largest luggers, wallowing under massive cargoes of French contraband, dropped anchor at Bourne Bottom, where teams of landers disburdened them of immense quantities of brandy, tobacco, silk and other luxury goods. The various boxes, barrels, kegs and bales were loaded onto wagons and ponies that then began to wend their way inland across the heath, before dispersing towards Gulliver's many houses and other hiding places. The smuggler himself, astride his best horse, rode at the head of the convoy, which, according to an onlooker, extended to a distance of two miles. With this superb *tour de force* he brought to an end a career of unparalleled success.

It has often been questioned why Gulliver was apparently able to come and go almost as he wished. His 'white wigs', too, avoided arrest or imprisonment. In Lyme Regis, while waiting for instructions from their master, they often gathered in large numbers at a hostelry less than a hundred yards along the front from the Custom House. It should be remembered, though, that customs officers were then relatively few in number and had to cover excessively large areas. An efficient organizer, deploying even a small number of men, could make rings round them. Their powers of arrest were also limited: smugglers not only had to be caught redhanded, but taken into custody. Three or four officers were hardly a match for fifteen or so of Gulliver's 'white wigs'. An officer's pay could be as low as £20 a year; it is not surprising that they frequently supplemented their incomes with bribes which, to them, would have been substantial sums, yet to somebody as rich as Gulliver, just small change. However, the chief reason why he enjoyed what almost amounts to immunity from prosecution is thought to stem from his having discovered, while in France, a plot to assassinate George III. He immediately conveyed this news to the king, whose spies investigated the allegation and, finding it true, exposed the plotters. In gratitude, George is thought to have exclaimed, 'Let Gulliver smuggle as much as he likes!'

In 1817 he moved to his final home, now known as Gulliver's House, in West Borough, Wimborne Minster. His daughter Elizabeth, who had married a banker, William Fryer, lived in the same street; Fryer's bank was eventually absorbed by the National Provincial. His granddaughter Ann, who also married a banker, lived in East Borough. Among his descendants, one became the first Lieutenant-Governor of Burma and two were knighted. Gulliver himself achieved official status towards the end of his life by being elected a churchwarden of Wimborne Minster, which is striking proof of the permissive attitude that then existed towards smuggling. His last years were spent in comfort and luxury; he was often to be seen taking the air in a Bath chair propelled along the street by a faithful retainer. He died on 13 September 1822 at the age of seventy-seven and was buried in Wimborne Minster; his memorial stone, worn down with the passing of time, can be seen in the central aisle, beneath the western tower.

He left a fortune so dazzling that it still casts a warm glow over many branches of the family tree. His will, as meticulous and detailed as his smuggling operations, runs to about 12 000 words; the range of property, land, investments and other assets is sufficiently remarkable for this document to have become a model text that is regularly scrutinized by law students. In his best years his gross annual income may have exceeded £50 000. If we take into account the low rates of tax that prevailed in those days, together with more than a century and a half's inflation, we can see that, by modern standards, Gulliver was a multimillionaire.

There are a number of testaments to the man's enterprising career. We have already come across a farm and a house named after him, and on Eggardon Hill is Gulliver's Lane. Memorabilia are on display in the Priest's House Museum, Wimborne Minster and the Russell-Cotes Art Gallery and Museum, Bournemouth; an interesting collection is also kept at Chettle House, near Sixpenny Handley. Of possible connections, the most appealing is the Lilliput district, directly north of Sandbanks, on the shore of Poole Harbour. The name is believed to derive from Lilliput Farm, which existed in that area since about the 1780s. Was it so called because, in allusion to Jonathan Swift's *Gulliver's Travels* (1726), it represented somebody's tiny kingdom, or did Isaac Gulliver once own the farm and merrily christen it thus? Perhaps, one day, we shall know.

9

Jack Rattenbury

The West Country's most famous smuggler is Jack Rattenbury. We know a great deal about his activities because a book of his memoirs was published. This was printed in Sidmouth in 1837, being compiled from his diaries and journals by a ghostwriter with whom he appears to have collaborated closely. There seems little doubt that the writer was John B. Smith, who resided at Colyton, four miles north of Beer, where Rattenbury spent most of his life. Smith, somewhat surprisingly, was a poet and, even more surprisingly, a Unitarian minister. His books of poetry include *The Solitary Seagull, Shute Park* and *Seaton Beach,* which is a single poem running to more than a hundred pages. From 1830 he was pastor of the Unitarian Congregational Church of George's Meeting in Colyton. Although we may find it curious for a clergyman to wish to be associated with a smuggler, it should be remembered that only a dozen miles to the west of Colyton, at East Budleigh, the Reverend Ambrose Stapleton was then vigorously engaged in smuggling activities; moreover, his predecessor, the Reverend Matthew Mundy, had followed the same calling, and their manse, Vicar's Mead, was honeycombed with concealed passages and secret recesses.

The material with which Smith prefaces Rattenbury's supposed account of his life does not augur well for the rest of the book. The Isle of Wight is rendered latinately as 'the rocky shores of Vecta', and a quotation from *Othello*, Act 1, Scene 3, lurches forward in so progressively garbled a state that Smith can bring it to an end only by manufacturing a line of his own. In addition, Rattenbury is described as 'The Rob Roy of the West', which is based on nothing more than a greeting offered by Sir William Pole when the smuggler called on him at Shute House in May 1827: 'Here is Rob Roy come again!' It is not quite clear what the baronet meant. In the introduction to his celebrated novel, Sir Walter Scott related that

> Rob Roy avoided every appearance of cruelty, and it is not averred that he was ever the means of unnecessary bloodshed, or the actor in any deed which could lead the way to it. His schemes of plunder were contrived and executed with equal boldness and sagacity, and were

> almost universally successful, from the skill with which they were laid, and the secrecy and rapidity with which they were executed. Like Robin Hood of England, he was a kind and gentle robber, and, while he took from the rich, was liberal in relieving the poor . . . We are not, however, to suppose the character of this distinguished outlaw to be that of an actual hero . . . On the contrary, as is common with barbarous chiefs, Rob Roy appears to have mixed his professions of principle with a large alloy of craft and dissimulation, of which his conduct during the civil war is sufficient proof.

This represents the generally accepted view of Rob Roy, but it would certainly not suffice as a description of Jack Rattenbury, who neither led a band of robbers nor gave to the poor. What they did have in common, though, was an extraordinary ability to escape from practically any predicament. In his book *Rob Roy MacGregor*, W.H.Murray writes, 'Rob Roy became in the public mind a legendary character, whom neither kings, generals, dukes, sheriffs, nor their armies, were able to capture for the gallows.' Rattenbury's similar elusiveness was what made him also a figure of legend.

After such an unpromising introduction to the memoirs, one might well embark on the main body of the book with dwindling enthusiasm. But Smith at once finds what is obviously his true form, as he loses himself in his subject's stirring life and produces a direct colourful narrative, entirely free of the moralizing that mars many similar works. One such autobiography, written by the Cornish smuggler Harry Carter, who extricated himself from many plights, yet eventually succumbed to Methodism, opens in an atmosphere of religious fervour that contrasts vividly with the almost amoral straightforwardness of the Colyton minister.

> As it have been imprest upon my mind for sevral years to take a memorandum of the kind dealings of God to my soul, in particular these laste two or three years, I have been persuaded by sevral of my friends, in particular Mr. Wormsley and Geo. Carter. I have thought in general it would be so weak that no person of sense would ever publish it to the world, notwithstanding, this morning being 20 of Dec$^{r.}$ 1809, I have taken up my pen, and may the Lord bring past things to my remembrance yest as they are, and if published to the world, may the Lord make it a blessing to every soul that read and hear it for Christ's sake, amen, amen.

Smith, as Rattenbury, simply plunges in, 'I was born at Beer, in the county of Devon, in the year 1778', and this is where we shall now join them both.

Jack Rattenbury was baptized on 18 October 1778. His father was a cordwainer (shoemaker) who left Jack's mother during her pregnancy, boarded a ship and was never heard of again. His mother supported herself and the baby by selling fish. Jack first went to sea when he was about nine, on his uncle's fishing boat, but managed to lose the rudder and was thrashed with a rope. He joined a Brixham fisherman as an apprentice, endured a further year of floggings and transferred to another boat at Bridport. When his master absconded to avoid conscription, the boy went to Torquay, where he enlisted on the privateer *Dover*, destined for the Azores.

> . . . even now, notwithstanding the lapse of years, I can recall the triumph and exultation whch rushed through my veins as I saw the shores of my native country recede, and the vast ocean opening before me; I was like a bird which had escaped from the confinement of the cage, and obtained the liberty after which it panted. I thought on some who had risen from the lowest to the highest posts, from the cabin boy to the admiral's flag; I wished to make a figure on the stage of life, and my hopes and expectations were restless and boundless like the element around me.

However, three futile months passed without any excitements; the crew were put on short allowance, the provisions were nearly at an end. Then,

> . . . we spied a ship to our leeward, and it was agreed to bear down upon her, in order to ascertain what she was; when we came up with her we perceived that she carried English colours, and our captain ordered all hands to go aloft and to give her three cheers. But as we were preparing to do so, to our great surprise and alarm, the crew hauled down their English colours and hoisted French ones, and immediately fired two shots at us, one of which went through our jib, and the other between our fore and main-mast. As the French ship mounted twenty-six guns, resistance was out of the question, and escape impossible, and we were obliged quietly to submit to our fate. The captain then sent a boat alongside our vessel to take the crew on board his ship, who were immediately ironed two and two, and sent down into the lower hold, where they found fifty other English prisoners who had been captured out of a South Sea merchantman. Being a boy, I was ordered to stand by a gun on the quarter deck, where I remained till five o'clock in the evening, when I was sent below to join my companions. The next morning two other boys were taken out of irons, and they, together with myself, were appointed to attend to the prisoners, each having a certain number allotted to his charge. Nothing could be more truly deplorable than the situation of these poor men, through the badness of their provisions and the narrow space in which they were confined, insomuch that though a boy, I often felt more for them than for myself, and used to watch every opportunity when the French sailors were on deck, to take all the provisions I could procure, and carry them below to my own shipmates, in order to mitigate their sufferings as far as I was able.

A fortnight later they reached Bordeaux, where the English sailors were imprisoned. The fourteen-year-old boy, having endeared himself to his captors and been granted a small measure of latitude, eventually duped a sentry with a worthless short-term pass, made his way from the prison to the harbour and boarded an American vessel. He was given refuge, but, because of the French embargo on foreign shipping, the boat had to stay in Bordeaux for a year. It then voyaged to New York where he discovered a brig bound for Le Havre and was taken on as cook and cabin boy. In Le Havre he found similar employment on a Boston merchantman apparently heading for London. However, the ship sailed to Copenhagen and thence to Göteborg. Six weeks later it started on the return passage to France, but was blown on to the coast of Norway near Kristiansand. The weather continued so stormy that the boat was forced to take shelter there for three months. At last reaching Le Havre again, Jack obtained a post on a boat making for Guernsey. From there he crossed to Beer, 'where I had the pleasure of seeing my mother, and the friends of my early youth, who were all overjoyed to see me, and not a little pleased with hearing me relate the adventures I had met with.'

Young Rattenbury was now almost sixteen. 'I remained at home about six months, part of which was occupied in fishing, but I found the employment very dull and tiresome after the roving life I had led; and as the smuggling trade was then plied very briskly in the neighbourhood, I determined to try my fortune in it.' He had some success, but four months later he took a position on a square-rigger that was sailing from Bridport to Tenby, in South Wales, to pick up a cargo of anthracite.

> At eight o'clock the captain set the watch, and it was my turn to remain below; at twelve I went on deck, and continued till four, when I went below again, but was scarcely dropped asleep, when I was aroused by hearing the captain exclaim, 'Come on deck, my good fellow! Here is a privateer, and we shall all be taken.' When I got up, I found the privateer close alongside of us. The captain hailed us in English, and asked us from what port we came, and where we were bound. Our captain told the exact truth, and he then sent a boat with an officer in her, to take all hands on board his own vessel, which he did, except myself and a little boy, who had never been to sea before. He then sent his prize-master and four men on board our brig, with orders to take her into the nearest French port. When the privateer was gone, the prize-master ordered me to go aloft and loose the main-top gallant sail. When I came down, I perceived that he was steering very wildly, through ignorance of the coast, and I offered to take the helm, to which he consented, and directed me to steer south-east by south. He then went below, and was engaged in drinking and carousing with his companions. They likewise sent me up a glass of grog occasionally, which animated my spirits, and I began to conceive a hope not only of escaping, but also of being revenged on the enemy. A fog too came on, which befriended the

design I had in view; I therefore altered the course to east by north, expecting that we might fall in with some English vessel. As the day advanced, the fog gradually dispersed, and the sky getting clearer, we could perceive land; the prize-master and his companions asked me what land it was; I told them it was Alderney, which they believed, though at the same time we were just off Portland. We then hauled our wind more to the south until we cleared the Bill of the island; soon after we came in sight of land off St Alban's [on the Isle of Purbeck]: the prize-master then again asked what land it was which we saw; I told him it was Cape La Hogue [Cap de la Hague, near Cherbourg]. My companions then became suspicious and angry, thinking I had deceived them, and they took a dog that had belonged to our captain, and threw him overboard in a great rage, and knocked down his house. This I supposed to be done as a caution, and to intimate to me what would be my own fate if I had deceived them. We were now within a league of Swanage, and I persuaded them to go on shore to get a pilot: they then hoisted out a boat, into which I got with three of them, not without serious apprehension as to what would be the event; but hope animated, and my fortunate genius urged me on. We now came so near to the shore that the people hailed us, and told us to keep further west. My companions now began to swear, and said the people spoke English: this I denied, and urged them to hail again; but as they were rising to do so, I plunged overboard, and came up the other side of the boat: they then struck at me with their oars, and snapped a pistol at me, but it missed fire. I still continued swimming, and every time they attempted to strike me, I made a dive and disappeared. The boat in which they were now took in water, and finding they were engaged in a vain pursuit, and endangering their own lives and safety, with little chance of being able to overtake me, they suddenly turned round, and rowed away as fast as possible to regain the vessel. Having got rid of my foes, I put forth all my efforts to get to the shore, which I at last accomplished, though with great difficulty. In the mean time the men in the boat reached the brig, and spreading all their canvass, bore away for the French coast. Being afraid that they would get off with the vessel, I immediately sent two men, one to the signal house at St Alban's, and another to Swanage, to obtain all the assistance they could to bring her back.

Fortunately, there was at the time in Swanage Bay a small cutter, belonging to his majesty's customs, called the Nancy, commanded by Captain Willis; and as soon as he had received the information, he made all sail after them; but I was not on board, not being able to reach them in time, which was a great disappointment to me. The cutter came up with the brig, about nine o'clock in the evening, and by retaking, brought her into Cowes the same night, where the men were put in prison. Captain Willis then sent me a letter, stating what he had done,

> and advising me to go as quickly as possible to the owners, and inform them of all that had taken place. This I did without delay, and one of them immediately set off for Cowes, when he got her back by paying salvage. When the whole transaction was over, I was not a little elated at the part I had taken in it, but I never received any reward for the service I had rendered, either from the owners, or from any other quarter . . . .

No sooner had Rattenbury rejoined the brig than he was press-ganged into the Royal Navy, submitting to a month's imprisonment before 'volunteering'. After a short cruise to the Channel Islands, he jumped ship at Spithead, went by fishing smack to Portland, and made his way back to Beer.

For the next five years he occupied himself with fishing, smuggling, freighting and victualling. In February 1799 he enlisted on a Topsham brig headed for Newfoundland. They put into Waterford for provisions, returned there for repairs and arrived at St John's after three weeks' passage. The summer and autumn were spent in netting and curing a bumper haul of cod. In November they set out for Portugal to sell their catch, but, a dozen miles from Oporto, were nabbed by a Spanish privateer and taken to Vigo. Rattenbury became friendly with the prize-master, who granted him his freedom and gave him a mule for the journey over the border to Viana do Castelo. From there he travelled to Oporto and was provided with a berth on a schooner going to Guernsey. However, heavy gales drove the boat into the Irish Sea; it anchored at Glandore, then ploughed along the coast to Baltimore, on the southernmost tip of Ireland, where repairs were undertaken. Venturing out after several days, it was again blown off course and took refuge in Cork Harbour. It finally tied up in Guernsey some three weeks later. He then went on board a packet embarking for Weymouth and reached Beer the following day. Once more, he had been away for over a year.

Absence possibly made his heart grow fonder, for on 17 April 1800, less than a month after his return, he married his sweetheart, Anna Partridge, and they settled in Lyme Regis. Unable to find satisfactory employment, he signed up as a privateersman on board a lugger that sailed for the Azores in the following month. The voyage proved totally fruitless; they did not dock at Weymouth until after Christmas. For the next few years he was occupied principally with piloting and victualling. During that time he was again picked up by a press-gang, but managed to escape. In 1804 he moved back to Beer, where he concentrated on smuggling. He was once nearly caught when tracked to a public house, but eluded the customs officer by climbing up the chimney and hiding for an hour. In February 1805 he had another go at privateering, yet with no more success than on his previous expeditions. This time a tender overturned and several lives were lost; Rattenbury, too, might have perished, had he not been such a powerful swimmer. 'I determined never again to engage in privateering, a resolution which I have ever since kept, and of which I have never repented.' After arriving back in Beer in August

1805, he devoted his time to fishing and smuggling. He was captured that summer on a trip to Christchurch, but managed to escape and even to rescue his companions. During the following spring he was again taken, on his way back from Alderney, and again broke free, reaching Beer after a journey by foot, on horseback and in a fishing smack. In July 1806 the law at last caught up with him; he appeared before the magistrates in Falmouth and was sentenced to prison. On the road to Bodmin Gaol, at Indian Queens, he got away from his escort and went to Newquay. From there he travelled by horse to Mevagissey and by boat to Budleigh Salterton, before walking home to Beer. Later that year he was once more press-ganged and put on a frigate that sailed from Portsmouth to Cork, where he succeeded in leaving the ship and ran off into the countryside. He hired a gig from a farmer, drove to Youghal and, by good fortune, found a vessel bound for Weymouth. Five days later he was in Beer. Soon afterwards he rather blotted his copybook by undertaking, for £100, to ferry across to Cap de la Hague four French officers who had just broken out of prison in Tiverton. The officers were recaptured at a house near the beach in Beer; Rattenbury had to appear before the magistrates and was lucky to be let off with a caution after protesting that he understood the Frenchmen were actually Channel Islanders. A little later he found himself in what was perhaps his tightest situation, when he was suddenly cornered in a tavern by a squad of soldiers detailed to arrest him for desertion from the Royal Navy. He at once jumped into the cellar.

> I then threw off my jacket and shirt, to prevent any one from holding me; and, having armed myself with a reaphook, and a knife which I had in my pocket, I threw myself into an attitude of defence at the entrance, which was a half-hatch door, the lower part of which I shut, and then declared that I would kill the first man who came near me, and that I would not be taken from the spot alive. At this the sergeant was evidently terrified, but he said to his men, 'Soldiers, do your duty, advance and seize him'; to which they replied, 'Sergeant, you proposed it: take the lead, and set us an example, and we will follow.' No one, however, offered to advance, and I remained in the position which I have described, for four hours, holding them at bay. Not knowing how to act, the sergeant at last sent to Lieutenant Durall; but before he arrived, some women ran into the house, with a story that there was a vessel drifted ashore, and a boy in danger of being drowned. This tale they told in such a natural manner, that it attracted the attention of the sergeant and his men; and, while they were listening and making inquiries about it, I jumped over the hatch, and rushed through the midst of them, without their being able to lay fast hold of me, in consequence of the precaution which I had taken to lay aside my clothes. I then ran towards the beach, and some men got me into a boat, and conveyed me on board the vessel, where I immediately hoisted the colours.

Beer harbour in 1829; many of Jack Rattenbury's smuggling expeditions began and ended here, not always profitably

Not long afterwards he went to the aid of a boat in distress and piloted her to safety, after riding out a terrible storm. Since the boat happened to be a troopship carrying men of the Prince of Wales' Volunteers Regiment, this courageous act won him golden opinions in the right places. He was rewarded with twenty guineas and a further guinea to pay for the printing of a handbill describing how he had saved the soldiers' lives. He presented copies of the handbill to the lord of the manor, Lord Rolle, and to the equally influential Lady Rolle. A week later he was given to understand that the Royal Navy had decided to turn a blind eye to his desertion.

He continued for a time to smuggle, yet with only moderate success, achieving little financial security. Towards the end of 1809 he became a publican. 'At first the house appeared to answer pretty well, but after being in it for two years, I found that I was considerably gone back in the world; and that my circumstances, instead of improving, were daily getting worse, for all the money I could get by fishing and piloting went to the brewer, with whom the business was confined; and the times were very hard, trade and commerce being in a state of great stagnation, and little or no prospect of their revival. Thus situated, and not knowing what else to do, I now returned to my old trade of smuggling . . . .' He was soon in trouble again, being intercepted on his way back from Alderney by a Royal Navy cruiser.

> A very warm chase then ensued, in the course of which, she fired twenty-four cannon-shot at us; in consequence of which we were

> thrown into the greatest alarm, not knowing whether we had fallen in with a French privateer, or an English vessel. About half-past ten o'clock in the morning they came so near to us, that finding that there was no hope of escaping, we hauled down all our sails. The crew, however, still kept up an incessant fire of small arms upon us, several of which went through our binnacle and bulwarks, and the sails we had hauled down. All the men except myself were below, and in the midst of this tremendous volley, I escaped without a single wound; a circumstance on which I have since reflected, not without wonder; but my mind was then in such a state of excitement, that I thought but little of the danger to which I was exposed.
>
> When the captain came within hail of us, he called out, 'You rascals, I will put you all on board a man-of-war.' To his great disappointment, however, upon inspecting our vessel, he found nothing on board her, except a pint of gin in a bottle; but he detained the vessel; and, having put myself and my companions on board his own brig, took us into Brixham.

Rattenbury told him, 'You have behaved towards me most shamefully: you have taken my vessel on the high seas, and detained it, though you found nothing on board to justify you in doing so; and it is, I conceive, an act of piracy.' This accusation seems merely to have stiffened the captain's resolve to hold on to his prisoners. A week later Anna Rattenbury and other wives were allowed on board to see their husbands. A plan was hatched and on the following morning the women returned in a larger, better boat. Once alongside, they began to climb onto the brig. Their men jumped down to assist them, and, as soon as they had helped them out, they shoved off and rowed away strongly. Shots were fired and the sail was brought down; the boat safely reached the shore, where the smugglers started scrambling up the cliffs. When he had reached the top, Rattenbury 'looked back, but could see no one. I then took off my jacket, and left it behind me, thinking that if they met with it, they would suppose that I had thrown it off to facilitate my speed in getting away. After this, I rolled myself down the cliffs, not far from where we landed.' He then made for Torquay and thence to Beer. Two of his mates were recaptured and transported to the West Indies.

In November 1813 he gave up his public house 'in consequence of bad debts, several misfortunes, and the general stagnation of trade . . . My situation was now a very deplorable one, for I had a wife and four children to support; my money was all gone, there was scarcely any thing to be done in smuggling, and I had nothing left but a boat, in which myself and my eldest son were accustomed to go fishing, that being the employment in which we were engaged during the summer, and in which we met with very indifferent success.' Soon afterwards the boat was smashed to pieces in a gale. Bad weather, however, also provided him with the opportunity of improving his lot, for he was called upon to pilot to safety a number of vessels that found themselves in difficulties. On one such occasion he was paid £100 by the captain of a stricken Dutch galiot. Some customs-house officers reached the boat just before him, but were turned down in favour of Rattenbury. They later had the audacity to take him to court, demanding a share of his honorarium, but the magistrates quickly threw out the case. The customs men thereafter went out of their way to harass him on any pretext. In August 1815 he was prosecuted for bringing into the country a single bottle of gin, which he tossed into the sea after being commanded to surrender it to an officer. The judge dismissed the charge, deeming it frivolous and vexatious.

Around this time his smuggling ventures began to meet with more satisfactory results. He bought a half-share in two fishing sloops, purchased another outright and commissioned the building of a longboat in Cherbourg. Two of these vessels were completely wrecked, but he continued to prosper. His health, though, was beginnning to give him trouble. During the early months of 1818, when still only thirty-nine, he was laid up with a severe attack of gout; exactly two years later he was again incapacitated for almost the same length of time. In May 1820 he tried his hand at something completely new, skippering a pleasure yacht for a wealthy gentleman who had decided to spend the summer cruising with his friends in the Channel. They went to Sidmouth, Dartmouth, Brixham and other resorts, visiting the Channel Islands as well. In Guernsey Rattenbury became extremely ill, but his employer made sure he received the best attention. 'I can never forget the kindness and humanity with which he provided medical assistance for me, and supplied my various wants till I recovered.'

In 1821, he had another serious brush with a patrol vessel.

> . . . the captain attempted to come on board, but we told him to keep off. They again attempted to board us, but we shoved her off with a boat-hook; upon which, she dropped astern of our vessel, and began to fire at us. The first shot carried away our main halliards, and down came the sails: she then rode up again under the stern, and then renewed the fire; upon which one of our men hove a shy-stone at the boat, which pitched on the gunnel instead of going into it. They still kept firing, and several shots went through the counter and companion of the vessel, and they continued to fire till their ammunition was quite exhausted, upon which he rode up alongside the vessel, and I asked him what he wanted; he recollected my voice, and said, 'Master Rattenbury, you had better let me come alongside quietly.' I then prevailed on the crew, English and French, to do so. He then came on board and searched the vessel, but found nothing.

A few days later, Rattenbury's luck ran out; the result was six months' imprisonment in Exeter. He served a further term, of fifteen months, in Exeter in 1826–7, having been arrested off the coast near Dawlish. The prison meals displeased him. 'Not being satisfied with the jail allowance, which consisted

A copy of the only known portrait of Jack Rattenbury; the original appeared as the frontispiece to his memoirs, published in 1837, when he was fifty-nine

of twenty-two ounces of bread every morning, and ten pounds of potatoes and a pound of pork per week, I wrote a letter to the board for my pay instead; and, in consequence of it, on the 15th of February [1826], received an order to be paid 4½d. per day.'

In the summer of 1827 he twice travelled to London, at the request of Beer's leading citizens, to provide information in both the House of Commons and the House of Lords to committees concerned with the building of a harbour at Beer and the construction of a canal that would start there and ultimately reach across to the Bristol Channel. That he should be selected to represent his village in these matters is testimony to his standing as man and mariner. His timetable during this period was:

5 April	Release from Exeter Gaol
14 June	Attendance at the House of Commons
c.28 June	Smuggling expedition
8 July	Attendance at the House of Lords

While in London he was frequently in the company of Lord Rolle, calling upon him at Westminster Hall and at his house in Grosvenor Square. Lord

Rolle initiated the harbour and canal schemes in 1820 and seems to have had Rattenbury in mind for an important post connected with them; yet, in the long run, it all came to nothing. He returned home in July 'with blue ribbons in my hat, and a merry heart, from the expectation of deriving great advantage from the passing of the act; but was sadly disappointed in the result, for notwithstanding the bill was passed, the project was entirely dropped.'

When he was asked by a member of the House of Commons committee how he earned his living, 'I told him sometimes fishing, sometimes piloting, and sometimes smuggling.' To these pursuits he now returned for the next two years. However, in 1829, through the sponsorship of Lord Rolle, he joined the crew of the *Tartar*, a revenue cutter operating in the Solent. Having served on this vessel for under a year, he became mate on a schooner transporting a consignment of manganese whose destination was Kilmarnock. As soon as the cargo had been discharged, he journeyed to Banff and worked for two months on a trawler fishing for herring in the North Sea.

In November 1831 he and his crew were captured by the Preventative Water Guard in Seaton Bay. The crew consisted of his son William, aged thirty, and two other Beer men, Isaac Lane, a fisherman, and William Abbot, a labourer. They were tried in Lyme Regis and found guilty of smuggling. The sentence was a fine of £100 and fourteen months' imprisonment in Dorchester Gaol. Following his release early in 1833, Rattenbury, now in his fifty-fifth year, resumed his smuggling operations, but with diminished success, partly because the customs men seemed more frequently to be shadowing him whenever he took to the water, and partly because attacks of gout increasingly curtailed his own participation. In January 1836 he decided to call it a day after narrowly escaping from an ambush near Torquay.

> Thus ended my career as a smuggler – a career which, however, it may be calculated to gratify a hardy and enterprising spirit, and to call forth all the latent energies of the soul, is fraught with difficulty and danger; in following which, many and various have been the expedients to which I have had recourse, in order to escape detection, baffle pursuit, and elude the vigilance of those indefatigable picaroons which every where line our coasts.

Among the more unusual expedients to which he resorted was bringing into the country a decidedly succulent goose, 'but I was too well aware of the value of the stuffing to part with it, for instead of onions and sage, it consisted of fine lace.' In December 1839 Queen Victoria's predominantly lace wedding dress was ordered from Beer seamstresses, at a cost of £1000; she would probably not have been amused to learn the process by which the material sometimes entered her realm.

Although Jack Rattenbury retired from smuggling, William continued in the family business, which resulted in his prosecution at Exeter Assizes on 23 March 1836. Jack appeared on his son's behalf, maintaining that William had been nowhere near Budleigh Salterton, the scene of the supposed crime, but at home in Beer. When cross-examined by Mr Serjeant Bompas (who was the original of Serjeant Buzfuz in Charles Dickens's *Pickwick Papers,* published in 1837), he more than held his own; according to *Trewman's Exeter Flying-Post,* 'This witness convulsed the court with laughter.' He also had some serious remarks to make: 'I am an honest man, and brought up my children in an honourable way, to say the Lord's Prayer, the Creed, and the Ten Commandments . . . I have always been beliked by every man. I have been a smuggler, but I would not take a false oath to save my wife or my child.' William was nevertheless found guilty and sentenced to transportation for seven years. However, the verdict was later overturned, and a royal pardon was granted.

The memoirs conclude with the prospect of further court proceedings.

> Since I left off smuggling, I have been principally engaged in fishing and piloting, but have lately entered into an engagement for conveying the blue lias lime, and the stone, for the harbour which is in contemplation at Sidmouth. In the exercise of my profession as a pilot, I have, under Divine Providence, been instrumental in saving many vessels from being wrecked. An instance of this kind occurred a short time ago, which is likely to occasion me some little inconvenience; for after I had succeeded in saving the vessel, a person who went on board told the captain that I and those who assisted me were the very men who would rob him, which so roused my passions, that I instantly struck him a blow; and I have since been served with a summons to appear before the magistrates; but as I took no notice of that, I have received another.

A postscript adds, 'The Smuggler gratefully acknowledges the kindness of the Right Hon. LORD ROLLE, who now allows him one shilling per week for life.' Some commentators have inferred from this statement that Lord Rolle is likely to have had an interest in Rattenbury's operations, perhaps financing them. This seems possible. However, the Rolle family were patrons of Beer, which was a desperately poor village. Lady Rolle endowed the school there and carried out numerous acts of charity. Lord Rolle provided pensions annually for at least a dozen elderly fisherman, so there was nothing unusual about the weekly shilling, particularly for a man whom his lordship obviously liked.

Jack Rattenbury died at the age of sixty-five and was buried in Seaton churchyard, close to the north transept, on 28 April 1844; the exact site of his grave is no longer known. Unlike his contemporary Isaac Gulliver, he bequeathed no fortune to his descendants; as far as we can tell, he left nothing. But his spirited adventures and winning personality have brought pleasure to many, and will continue to do so. He makes appearances in several works of fiction, notably *Twas in Trafalgar Bay* (1896) by Walter Besant and James Rice, *Parson Peter* (1900) by Arthur H. Norway and *Winifred* (1900) by Sabine Baring-Gould. The only surviving likeness we have of him is an engraving at the front of the memoirs; a large-scale reproduction hangs in the Fisherman's Bar of the Anchor Hotel, Beer. His coarse shirt is roomy and unbuttoned and, as one might expect from a man who has learnt to take precautions, he wears both belt and braces. The description of the smuggler Elzevir Block in the first chapter of J.Meade Falkner's novel *Moonfleet* (1898) shows a striking resemblance: 'He was a man of fifty, with a shock of grizzled hair, a broad but not unkindly face of regular features, and the finest forehead that I ever saw. His frame was thick-set, and still immensely strong; indeed, the countryside was full of tales of his strange prowess or endurance.'

In Beer, Rattenbury's cottage, which was built in 1820 from stone and other materials that he collected, still stands. The village commemorates him with Rattenbury Day. This is always the sixth Friday after the first Monday in August, which to those living in that part of the country apparently makes good sense. On Rattenbury Day, which began in 1978, the 200th anniversary of his birth, sweets and little gifts are given to children visiting the town, there is a coffee morning for pensioners, a treasure hunt and other games, and in the evening a fancy-dress dance. He would have liked it, wouldn't he?

Selected Bibliography

Baring-Gould, S. *Devon* (London, 1899)

——— *A Book of Dartmoor* (London, 1900, new edition by Wildwood House, 1982)

——— *Devonshire Characters and Strange Events* (Bodley Head, 1908)

Bray, Anna Eliza *Fitz of Fitz-ford* (London, 1833)

——— *Traditions, Legends, Superstitions, and Sketches of Devonshire* (London, 1838)

Byles, C. E. *The Life and Letters of R. S. Hawker* (Bodley Head, 1906)

Coxhead, J. R. W. *Smuggling Days in Devon* (Raleigh Press, 1956)

Dunn, Waldo Hilary *R. D. Blackmore* (London, 1956)

Fuller, Thomas *The History of the Worthies of England* (London, 1662)

Guttridge, Roger *Dorset Smugglers* (Dorset Publishing Company, 1984)

Hawker, R. S. *Footprints of Former Men in Far Cornwall* (London, 1870)

Hippisley Coxe, Antony D. *A Book About Smuggling in the West Country* (Padstow, 1984)

Johnson, Charles *A General and True History of Highwaymen* (London, 1742)

Morley, Geoffrey *Smuggling in Hampshire and Dorset 1700–1850* (Newbury, 1983)

Rattenbury, John *Memoirs of a Smuggler* (Sidmouth, 1837)

Snell, F. J. *The Blackmore Country* (London, 1906)

Thornycroft, L. B. *The Story of the Doones* (Cider Press, now Books of Wessex, 1939)

Ward, H. Snowden *The Land of Lorna Doone* (London, 1925)

A Narration of the Bloudy Murthers Commytted by the Handes of Sir John Fites (London, 1605)

The Great Robbery in the West: or, The Inn-Keeper Turn'd Highwayman (London, 1678)

The History of John Gregg, and His Family of Robbers and Murderers (c. 1770)